From Frederic Remington's famous *Changing Horses*. This scene is probably the most accurately detailed of all Pony Express pictures.

PONY EXPRESS
— THE GREAT GAMBLE

by Roy S. Bloss

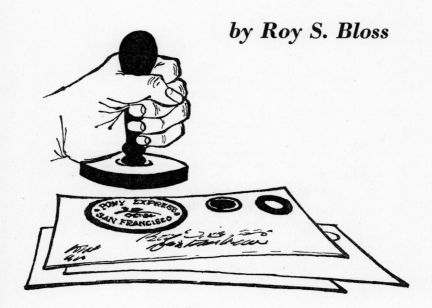

Berkeley **HOWELL-NORTH** *California*
1959

PONY EXPRESS—THE GREAT GAMBLE

Printed and bound in the United States of America by the Publisher.

Library of Congress Catalogue Card No. 59-15077.

Published by the Howell-North Press
1050 Parker Street, Berkeley 10, California

PREFACE

PROBABLY THE FINAL, complete and authentic word on the Pony Express will never be written.

For of all the notable episodes in United States history, few have been so scantily annotated as the horseback mail, the trail of which has been indelibly—but only grossly—etched in the panorama of American pioneering. Even the parade of Caesars, or the Gallic Wars, or our own Revolution—all in the days when historical narration lacked the incentive of the common man's literacy—even these events have been better documented and more accurately interpreted than the relatively recent Pony Express.

From the vantage point of retrospect one can see why. The Civil War, still America's most deadly conflict, became the blinding focal point of public attention, just as the fleet little ponies had chalked up a year's service freighting the California mail. By then the unique venture had assumed something of the flavor of an institution, and was comfortably taken for granted, while the great fratricide simply crowded it off the front page of public consciousness. After the war, the stress of reconstruction days, and the burgeoning development of the West, nearly relegated the Pony Express to the limbo of forgotten history.

Not until almost a half century after the last, unrecorded horse expressman delivered his *mochila* in Folsom, California, did the Pony Express begin to enjoy a literary renascence. But by then most of the principals, the riders and station keepers had passed from the scene.

That raised a problem for the early historians. Seemingly, few records of the 19-month mail service were then (or now, as a matter of fact) still extant. The living participants, pressed for their recollections, occasionally resorted to colorful embellishment or a self-serving memory. In several instances, the inexorable wear and tear of time caused buncombe to be offered as gospel.

It's disconcerting to read, for instance, in an entertaining piece on the Pony, that the stage realist, David Belasco, anticipated the overland horse mail "ten years before the Pony Express was thought of" by employing an express rider with a clumsy leather pouch in "The Girl of the Golden West." The play, unfortunately, wasn't staged until 1905—some 44 years after the Pony's demise.

Neither does the following charitable declaration of the owners' generosity, by the descendant of one of them, serve particularly well to point up the real purpose of a commercial venture founded on the profit motive:

> Dripping with hardship and adventure, with romance and story, no more beneficial nor magnanimous contribution, with such disaster to the owners, was ever made to the American people.

Such peccadillos, however, serve only to describe the challenge for today's reviewer. Annoyingly, he is confronted with a long list of unsure facts, or a vacuum of them, ranging all the way between the identity of the man who conceived the idea to the amount of money lost by the operators of this bold or foolhardy, praised and condemned experiment in private mail transport.

In this volume are presented the findings and analyses of a long detective hunt through new and old source material, and over a portion of the old Pony trail, in an endeavor to throw light on certain shadowed areas and to fill some complete voids with substance. Whenever sympathetic legend or nostalgic romance has threatened to collide with objective deduction (a recurring hazard in this lore-laden subject) objectiveness deliberately has been given the right-of-way. Admittedly, such arbitrariness may find disfavor among some devoted followers of the Pony; if so, their displeasure is risked with apologies.

For clarity and continuity, the main trail of the Pony Express story is here. But at numerous junction points stop-overs are made to discuss new detail more fully than might be expected in a purely narrative tale. This account, then, is offered to add upon and broaden, and to relate in what is hoped an unbiased view, the colorful story of a great gamble to breach the western frontier.

R.S.B.

ACKNOWLEDGMENTS

ANY EFFORT to relate a tale of history—unless it be with embellishments of fiction—primarily is a task of compilation. In fact, the labor of research, the analyzing and selection of useful data are apt to consume infinitely more time than putting the story on paper in what is hoped an interesting fashion. So it was here.

Many wonderful persons and organizations were helpful to me while wearing my compiler's hat. I would like to list them all but forbear because such a cataloging is an imposition on the general reader, and also might take on the appearance of a literary swagger stick—to borrow a phrase from George Hugh Banning. Suffice it to say that my gratitude is no less for the unnamed than the named.

Particularly, I am grateful for the generous aid received from the staff of Bancroft Library, that veritable treasure house of Western Americana. Without the courteous help and occasional advice on source material received there over a prolonged period of time this work would have been greatly hampered. Similar assistance is acknowledged from Mrs. Frances Hurd

Buxton, California Room, Oakland Public Library; Allan R. Ottley, California Section Librarian, The California State Library at Sacramento; and James deT. Abajian, Librarian, California Historical Society. The Library of Congress, the National Archives, the New York Public Library and the Nevada State Museum at Carson City all were sources of confirmation on research questions. Warm thanks are owed for the considerate hand extended by Librarian Robert O. Dougan and his staff of the Henry E. Huntington Library where I enjoyed productive digging for historical gold. Edgar B. Jessup, the noted philatelist, materially contributed to the illustrative scope of this book by generously making available a number of rare Pony Express covers.

Special appreciation is due Miss Irene Simpson, Director of the Wells Fargo Bank's History Room in San Francisco; and California State Senator Swift Berry, a noted authority on Pony affairs and Secretary of the Central Overland Pony Express Trail Association. Both unstintingly shared their knowledge and graciously offered suggestions. Through the friendly interest of William G. Huff, the sculptor and well-read student of western history, I was led to a most profitable meeting with Dr. Charles L. Camp of the University of California who, in turn, relayed me to the care and attention of Dale L. Morgan, author and historian. My thanks to each of them.

Finally, for her selfless patience and understanding, a purely personal debt of gratitude is owed an oft-forsaken partner, my wife.

ROY S. BLOSS

Alamo, California

CONTENTS

ILLUSTRATIONS

xi

Chapter One

THE FORERUNNERS

ALL OF SACRAMENTO was tingling with excitement. From Tenth to the levee, J Street had become a corridor of gesticulating, impatient onlookers, anxiously glancing eastward up the thoroughfare for *him*. Already a delegation of greeters had galloped to the outskirts of town. Strategically, they positioned themselves at the north side of Sutter's Fort, at the far end of J, the main route to the city.

Since early morning the citizens had joined in making elaborate—if somewhat delayed—preparations for a celebration. No one, apparently, had thought of planning a big to-do about a youngster on a horse until the suggestion was carried in the columns of the previous day's *Union*. But by mid-day local pride asserted itself, as public buildings and commercial establishments were gleefully decorated with flags.

A huge banner, opportunely found, was stretched across the intersection of Third and J, and store windows all along the street were plastered with paper signs that proclaimed the occasion. The Young America Volunteers of Engine House No. 6 trundled a cannon into the Tenth Street square and stood by. A block away, at Ninth Street, the No. 2 boys tugged an anvil into readiness, and so did Holmes and Andrews down at Sixth, near J. There would be no lack of noise to greet the coming rider.

In the waning light of the later afternoon, the tempo of excitement increased. Ladies swished through second-story doorways and onto balconies that overhung the street. Agile young chaps clambered for points of vantage on roofs and sheds, straining to catch the first glimpse of the parade.

Then there it was, a tiny cloud of dust, raised far up on J— but, no, this was a single rider, carrying a flag, probably an advance guard. It took just a moment for the main delegation to surge up behind, hot on his heels. They were a wildly galloping group, nearly a hundred riders strong, including 15 Sacramento Hussars, who came flying into town in a ragged band of pounding horseflesh, looking more like a charging posse than a welcoming parade. Along the sidewalk, the waiting crowd burst into a frenzy of yelling, handkerchief waving and arm flaying, as huge balls of dust billowed up from the racing hooves.

Somewhere, hopelessly lost in that mad, happy confusion was William Hamilton, Pony Express rider, making the first, historied, record-breaking delivery of transcontinental horse mail, only 11 days out of St. Joseph, Missouri. Even his mother probably couldn't have pointed him out in that blur of passing faces.

Suddenly, the air cracked with an ear-splitting boom of cannon. Quickly, there was another shot, then a third, finally nine in all, drowning out the shouting and yelling along the street. Immediately the No. 2 boys began sledge-hammering their anvil with a nine-stroke salute, and were mimicked, blow for blow, by Holmes and Andrews, who decided to add another chorus of 13 strikes for no explained reason.

Nearing Second Street, the racing band of horsemen reined in their mounts, and young Hamilton was easily discernible as he emerged from the crowd and trotted up to the telegraph office. From about 80 letters carried in his *mochila,* the agent removed those addressed to Sacramento, and entered on the waybill the time and date—5:30 p.m., April 14, 1860.

With greeters and onlookers crowding about, the rider remounted and dashed off to Rightmire's stables on K Street. He threw his *mochila* over the saddle of a fresh horse and galloped off to the dock of the river steamer *Antelope.* The Sacramento agent for the California Steam Navigation Company considerately had offered to delay departure of the 202-foot sidewheeler, providing Hamilton had come over the Sierras and reached Placerville by noon or shortly thereafter. He kept his word when the telegraph reported the expressman had left the mining town at 1:55 p.m.

Somewhere in Sacramento, probably between the telegraph office and the steamer dock, the *Union's* reporter button-holed Will Hamilton and elicited a report that the pioneer rider had left Sportsman Hall at 1:25 p.m. After leaving Placerville, he remounted fresh horses at Mud Springs, Mormon Tavern, Fifteen Mile House and Five Mile House, covering the last five miles into Sacramento in just 20 minutes.

So keyed up was local interest in the new mail service that other offers of kindly help had been made to the Pony Express, likely through the telegraph office. One such helping hand was extended by J. P. Robinson, superintendent of the Sacramento Valley Railroad. He proposed to make available a special locomotive and a tender at Folsom, California, to bring the rider into Sacramento. Although this idea "was responded to by a very decided nay," probably because the relay route was previously established, the railroad was to have the Pony as a regular customer before many weeks had passed.

For the nonce, however, all the glory belonged to the brave, intrepid riders who had halved the time between East and

West. Hamilton, as he led his horse up the *Antelope's* gang-plank, was a shining knight in the eyes of Sacramento, indeed of all California.

A whistle blew, a bell rang and the *Antelope* edged away from her berth. At her mast the red initials, "CSNCo.," blazoned on a white burgee, were no longer visible as the soft April night settled over the river.

The city's whopping celebration was like a timely popping of a relief valve in the steamed-up public opinion about Federal mail policies, under which Californians had been shoveling the political coal for over a half decade. Since early in 1855, when Congressman McDougall offered a bill for a daily overland mail, and Senator Gwin proposed a weekly express, the new state had fought, begged, pleaded and politicked for a fast mail service between her golden shores and the nostalgic "back home." In fact, the clamoring for mail in California began approximately when the wheels of the first arriving conestogas stopped rolling and the Argonauts alighted on the hallowed ground of promise and placer mining.

The first regular communication with the East was by way of ocean steamer, sailing monthly from New York on the arduous and hazardous voyage around Cape Horn. After January, 1855, when the railroad was completed across the Isthmus of Panama, the schedule was improved to semimonthly, providing a 22-day service. But the choosy settlers preferred neither the mode nor frequency of steamer mail. Only a direct route overland would meet the demands of these transplanted people, so utterly dependent, psychologically and materially, on civilization in the eastern states.

At the core of the argument was a new concept of the postal system. The doctrine long established on the principal of self-support was vigorously attacked by expansionist leaders who didn't view the Post Office as a well-run commercial venture that was supposed simply to deliver the mail and stay out of

Arrival of the first Pony Express at Sacramento. From the New York *Illustrated News.*

Pony Express Rider William Hamilton's arrival at San Francisco with the first mail was shown in this nocturnal drawing for the New York *Illustrated News.* The two sketches on this page, published on May 19, 1860, are the earliest known pictures of the Pony Express.

Sacramento fire company Young America No. 6 posed with all their regalia only a few months before the Pony Express started. Not evident is the cannon they used to welcome the first rider.

the red. They militantly declared that the postal service, particularly in the West, was a guarantor of civilization, a necessary helpmate for emigrants in keeping overland trails open and protected. There was much the Post Office could and must do in encouraging settlement and in functioning as vanguard of the railroad.

To be sure, the department had not wholly ignored the needs of California's new arrivals. In 1849, it had authorized a local post office in San Francisco which was established at the northeast corner of Washington and Stockton Streets. Col. J. W. Geary, officiating as postmaster, was accommodated in a private apartment of a dwelling house and provided boxes for his letter-hungry patrons. Another office was opened in Sacramento, but Postmaster Freeland was obliged to close the doors for two weeks in January, 1850, as the government had made no provision for the pay of clerks.

Then, in 1851, barely three years after gold was discovered in California, the overland mail advocates attained a more notable success. Major George Chorpenning, Jr., Indian fighter and trail blazer, departed Sacramento on May 1st for Salt Lake City, carrying about 75 pounds of mail on muleback under a new three-year $14,000-per-annum contract with the government.

He was to provide a monthly service, traveling the Humboldt River immigrant route, in 30 days. The muleback mail's initial trip, however, took 53 days, the contractor being delayed by snow in the Sierras and a stop in Carson Valley, where he staked out a quarter-section of land for a mail station. The site, present-day Genoa, at the eastern base of the mountains, became the first Mormon settlement in Nevada.

Although he was the original mail pioneer across the wilderness of mountain and desert, Chorpenning's fame is equally assured by the monumental physical hazards he encountered on the trail and, as a consequence, a chronic inability to give performance of his contract.

Absalom Woodward, his partner, who made the November, 1851, trip to Salt Lake City, was killed by the Indians, as were the four other men in his party. Chorpenning didn't find their remains—all mail was lost or destroyed—until the following May. Later that same month John Smith, an employee making the westward trip to Sacramento, arrived after "determined" Indian attacks on his party. He confirmed to the newspapers "the melancholy intelligence of the murder of Captain Woodward," and the publicity induced the rest of Chorpenning's help to desert him. So at Salt Lake City he lashed the mail bags to his mules and started out alone over the 900-mile route. Somehow he made it, after "successful conflicts" with hostile Indians and unrecorded physical hardship.

During the remaining time of his contract Chorpenning was obliged to change his route to San Pedro where mail from the East was sent by water, then back again to the Humboldt River trail, then south again via Los Angeles. The angry Postmaster General, as completely confused as anyone with the resulting irregularities and delays, cancelled the contract late in 1852, and signed another with W. L. Blanchard for $50,000—over three and a half times as much as Chorpenning received. Hearing this, Chorpenning hastened to Washington, explained everything, and returned home with his contract reaffirmed and his pay boosted to $30,000.

When renewal time came up in 1854, Chorpenning again was the low bidder. This time the route was changed to the San Diego-Salt Lake City route, with a provision for service to Carson Valley. His bid of $12,500 was ridiculously low. He had not only to supply wagons and the horses and their feed, but he had to furnish and subsist an escort of from four to ten men. The usual troubles, of course, happened. Raiding Indians reduced his stock and slowed travel, and his financial losses became acute. Once more he filed an application for relief in

Washington and a sympathetic Congress granted it. From 1856 his pay was increased to $30,000 for the balance of the contract.

Meanwhile, Californians in the northern part of the state were disgusted with the circuitous route which their mail was forced to take. From the populous mining districts it had to be carried by horse, then by river boat to San Francisco, thence via ocean steamer to southern California, where it was picked up by Chorpenning and toted back north to Salt Lake City. The Post Office couldn't hold out long against loud and vociferous criticism on the awkward arrangement and eventually capitulated. The 1858 contract, it announced, would follow the central route, between Salt Lake City and Placerville.

As before, public bids were taken and, as before, Chorpenning went in with the low figure. His contract was effective July 1, 1858, and provided for a semimonthly run of 20 days and pay at $65,000 a year. But in a flush of liberality the Post Office changed its mind before he began service and ordered the schedule improved to a weekly basis and the pay hiked to $130,000. That good news seemingly put the overland mail on a business-like footing.

On the strength of it Major Chorpenning bought 10 Concord coaches, large enough to carry the heavy mail of printed matter as well as letters. He surveyed a new, shorter route south of the Humboldt and established stations at convenient distances. Rosy, indeed, was the outlook for California.

Unfortunately, it didn't contemplate the vicissitudes of a changing Post Office policy. Beginning with the second year of the contract, service was slashed back to semimonthly trips and annual pay reduced to $80,000. Nonetheless, the plucky, stubborn Chorpenning continued to run his stages once a week, hauling occasional passengers at a $120 fare, and called for the mail every two weeks. That proved to be a fast road to poverty, and in the late summer of 1859 the line began to fall to pieces.

At Salt Lake City, the English traveler and writer, Sir Richard F. Burton, observed that "the drivers complained that the road agents, charged with paying them for 18 months, had expended the 'rocks' in the hells of San Francisco. The drivers notably evinced their race's power of self-government by seizing and selling off, by auction, wagons and similar moveable property."

In May, 1860, after two years of operation, the Post Office Department annulled the contract, alleging repeated service failures and the keeping of poor stock on the road. Chorpenning's mail-carrying career had ended, except as an angry claimant, seeking redress against the government.

Mail carriage east of Salt Lake City, if anything, was more poorly organized, just as underpaid, and was performed under conditions as primitive as those Chorpenning struggled with to the west. During the first two years of the Mormon settlement, the colonists were too busy carving a home out of the barren nothingness and too poor to undertake a responsible mail service. Correspondence with relatives back home was chanced by the occasional traveler to or from the Missouri River. In 1849 postal authorities finally conceded existence of the Mormon community, placing it on their maps, and opened an office under the management of J. L. Heywood. A bimonthly mail was authorized between Council Bluffs and Salt Lake City. Almond W. Babbitt was named carrier—at his own expense!

The first contractual arrangement, connecting Salt Lake City with the East, was made between the Post Office and Samuel H. Woodson of Independence, Missouri. Commencing July 1, 1850, he toted the mail on pack animals between the Missouri River and the Mormon capital for $19,500 per year. On August 1, 1851, Feramorz Little of Salt Lake City made a deal with Woodson as subcontractor over the western end of the route. Little and Woodson agreed to meet on the fifteenth of each month at Fort Laramie and exchange the east and west-bound mails. Associated with Little were Charles F. Decker and Eph- riam "Ephe" Hanks, a Mormon Danite who nine years later would serve overland stage travelers as station master at Big Canyon Creek.

His initial trip was a farcical epic. Fort Bridger, 124 miles distant, was the nearest speck of civilization east of Salt Lake City; beyond were 400 lonely miles to Fort Laramie. Years later, Little wrote that he and Hanks reached Fort Laramie nine days out of the Mormon town.

When they arrived the animals were so used up that they were unfit for the return trip. So the two men importuned the owner of a nearby ranch and obtained five wild, unbroken mules, the only stock available. These they wrestled to the ground, bound them and tied on blindfolds. Four of them they managed to work into a harness, and on the fifth one Ephriam Hanks put a saddle.

All was ready, the blindfolds were yanked off and the bind- ings cut. A lively performance commenced. Hanks took the lead, trying to assist in keeping the wagon on the road, but his mount "was guilty of all the antics that a wild Mexican mule is considered capable of performing under the circumstances." The wagon team kicked over the traces and over the tongue and back again. Mail and luggage danced about in a general jumble and some provisions were rudely dumped. But the pro- cession kept moving. At the end of the first day, a Mr. Dutton, whom Little and Hanks had the daring and rare nerve to take on as a passenger, probably sighed with relief that the animals had become "fairly manageable."

For the remainder of the Woodson contract the conduct of the mail was marked by extreme hardship, punctuated by Indian attacks, and irregular and unreliable service. In 1854, the route was awarded to W. M. F. Magraw. He fared no better. Suffering similar difficulties, he successfully applied, twice, to the House Committee on Post Offices and Post Roads for extra compensation. His second adjustment provided that the route would be thrown open to bid on August 18, 1856, two years before his original contract would terminate.

At this time the low bidder was Hiram Kimball, an agent of the Mormon leaders, who had visions of building up a great carrying company from the Missouri River to the Pacific Coast. Kimball's contract paid $23,000 per year for a monthly service in covered wagons, beginning October 16, 1856. By mid-summer of 1857, his contract was annulled after the "Utah War" was precipitated with the Mormons. Magraw may have been partially responsible for the cancellation, having written to President Buchanan a series of venom-filled letters on Mormonism. Service was resumed in October, with S. B. Miles, as contractor, receiving the increased pay of $32,000.

Soon there was another annulment, and a new contract was made with J. M. Hockaday & Company for a weekly service in four-mule wagons or stages at $190,000 per annum. A year later, in April, 1859, this contractor, as did Chorpenning, felt the axe of postal retrenchment and was obliged to reduce his schedule to semimonthly trips, a loss of $65,000 a year.

Congress was not entirely complacent about the willy-nilly, haphazard arrangements by which California and the West were getting mail. Following failure of the McDougall and Gwin attempts to establish a responsible post carriage in 1855, and another effort in 1856, opportunity knocked on the Congressional door in the guise of the annual Post Office Appropriation Bill of 1857. The expansionists succeeded in tacking on to it an amendment authorizing an overland mail, and the bill became law on March 3rd.

At the discretion of the Postmaster General, it provided for either a semimonthly, weekly, or semiweekly service for both mail and passengers, in four-horse coaches or spring wagons, on a schedule of 25 days. Land was to be given for the building of stations along the route—which was not specified.

Nine proposals for the contract were received by Postmaster General Aaron V. Brown. Being a southerner from Tennessee, he placed the hand of favor on the bid submitted by John Butterfield for a southern route from St. Louis, via El Paso; in fact, practically dictated to the politically wise contractor this "voluntary" choice of route. Butterfield's firm, the Overland Mail Company, was the creation of the country's four leading express companies—Adams, American, National and Wells Fargo. They held hopes of breaking the grip of the steamship lines on the bulk of passenger and mail traffic to the Pacific Coast.

As approved, the route extended from St. Louis to Little Rock, Arkansas, connecting with a branch to Memphis, thence proceeded to El Paso, joining and running parallel over James E. Birch's San Antonio & San Diego Mail Line as far as Yuma. There it turned north up California's interior valley to San Francisco.

Postmaster General Brown ordered up the service on a semi-weekly schedule, which called for pay at the rate of $600,000 a year. Butterfield fell to work, organizing the line, purchasing Concord spring wagons, hiring personnel, and building stations. By September 15, 1858, all was ready and the service began, with the mail simultaneously leaving St. Louis and San Francisco. From both ways it arrived on schedule amid general public acclaim. For the next two years the Overland mail was to keep on schedule, a notable improvement in western postal service and good evidence of John Butterfield's organizing talent. Something of the scope of the operation may be visualized from the *Alta California's* report that, in May, 1859, across half the continent, he had 165 stations staffed and operating, and had stocked them with 716 animals.

Each Concord wagon accommodated four sacks of mail, including one of newspapers, plus six passengers. The latter were treated with obvious unimportance, there being few civilized comforts provided for them along the 2,700-mile route.

Hardly had Butterfield's coaches begun to roll when a great hue and cry was raised. The Postmaster General was accused of choosing the southern route for the advantage of the South. Northerners and Westerners sneered at the line and called it the "Ox-Bow Route." They pointed to its great distance and the inordinate time required to complete a trip. They were, of course, advocates of the Central Route. Southerners replied that the Central Route was impossible to travel in winter and that claimants for it had ultimate designs on the Pacific Railroad, and that efforts on behalf of the Central Route were "an attempt to monopolize the benefits of this government for the North."

All the mounting furor and cavil tended to disguise the blessings in mail delivery that the last decade had brought to California. There were now three operative mail routes to the land of gold. The great bulk of mail continued to be carried via Panama steamer; the Central Route, still undeveloped, was an uncertain avenue primarily for local mail; and the efficient Butterfield operation, hauling both the through and local post, was the prelude of a promise to come.

Chapter Two

THE BIG IDEA

T HE OLD ADAGE that there's nothing new under the sun is especially apropos of the Pony Express. Everybody seems to have thought of the idea first. The record is confused with claims and counterclaims, and after a century's time still is unclear. Who said what and when has long been a matter of partisan debate; and while no one has yet emerged as the undisputed genius of the idea, the argument has illuminated interesting sidelights on the Pony's actual founding.

Senator William M. Gwin, Benjamin F. Ficklin, William H. Russell, John Scudder and Frederick A. Bee have all been listed as father to the thought. But for conception of a horse relay, *per se,* the laurels seem to go to Genghis Khan, conqueror of Tartary and China. Marco Polo reportedly wrote that he had established stations at 25-mile intervals, and that a single horseman would carry messages as far as 300 miles a day, probably apocryphal. A horseback mail of a much later age is cited by William Lightfoot Visscher. He noted that enterprising newspaper editors in New York and Boston employed express riders in the gathering of news and election returns between 1825 and 1830.

More pertinent, geographically, are the relay express services of Governor Stephen W. Kearny of California and of Major Chorpenning. General Kearny, as military governor of the new territory freshly wrested from Mexico, established a horse courier service of two soldiers, one at San Francisco and the other at San Diego. Starting on alternate Mondays, they kept a semi-monthly schedule, exchanging mail sacks at a convenient half-way point. Kearny's postal service gave transportation to both official communications and private letters without charge.

George Chorpenning, antedating the Pony Express by a little less than two years, established a one-time run along his new route south of the Humboldt River. When surveying the road in the fall of 1858, the idea of rapidly spanning the continent with President Buchanan's second annual message appealed to his fancy. Undoubtedly, it would be considered a gracious gesture for the mail contractor who, in July, had pocketed the largest contract ever awarded over the Salt Lake City-Placerville route. Of course, there would also be favorable political attention attracted to the Central Route.

Accordingly, he approached Hockaday on the plan, and between them they pooled $8,000 to defray expenses. Supposedly, he also contacted a special agent of the President, appointed to distribute copies of the speech to competing forms of transportation prior to general release of it to the newspapers. With these tentative arrangements concluded, fresh horses were posted about 18 miles apart all along the route, and everything put in a state of readiness.

Then chicanery intervened. Buchanan, without explanation, refused a copy of his message to go over the Central Route, permitting the speech to be carried only by the Butterfield line and ocean vessel. On December 6th a Tehuantepec steamer pulled out of New York and a Butterfield messenger dashed from St. Louis, each carrying an advance copy in a grand race to San Francisco. The Hockaday courier, who had come down to St.

Louis from St. Joseph, was left waiting empty handed. Not until eight days later, when he had returned to St. Joseph and there received a copy from a newspaper editor, was he able to spring away from the river bank and dash westward.

On Christmas night the swift Butterfield stage rolled into San Francisco, achieving the fastest time on record over any route, smartly beating the steamer by several days. The glory, however, was short lived. New Year's Day the record was shattered when Chorpenning's pony came flying into Placerville, only 17 days and 12 hours from St. Joseph, neatly trimming the Butterfield time by two days.

Endorsers of Senator William McKendree Gwin of California as initiator of the idea for *the* Pony Express draw their support from Gwin's own statements (which are conflicting) and on the writings of early Pony authors, such as W. F. Bailey, Visscher and Glenn Bradley. In Gwin's *Memoirs,* a detailed account of his political life dictated in the third person, there appears this statement, rarely quoted in full:

> On the 18th of January [1855], Mr. Gwin introduced a bill in the Senate to establish an express weekly mail between St. Louis, Mo., and San Francisco but did not succeed in getting it enacted into a law, but the enterprising mail contractor on the central route through Salt Lake established, at his own expense, and his own risk, this weekly mail, known as the pony express, which through the energy of Mr. B. F. Ficklin, who originated the scheme and carried it into operation, became a great success.

The clarity of meaning here, unfortunately, is befogged by a political speech he delivered in August, 1860, near the end of his second term of office. Addressing a Breckenridge Democrat meeting in Stockton, California, Gwin remarked that the Pony Express was "fostered and nurtured" by his own labor. It is to be remembered, though, that he was speaking for votes and very likely this smooth politician was merely heaping glory on his past efforts to procure an improved postal service.

In recent years writers have discredited earlier claims that Gwin and Ficklin discussed the possibility of a horse express during the fall of 1854. At that time the senator was journeying to Washington from California, riding much of the way on horseback. Ficklin is said to have been a companion over part of the route, and accounts of the ride describe him as general superintendent of Russell, Majors & Waddell. The validity of the claim is attacked with the reasoning that Russell, Majors & Waddell, out of which firm the Pony Express grew, did not embark on cross-country staging until 1859, and that Ficklin did not join the firm until 1860. Numerous records of the time, however, show that the multifarious business enterprises of Messrs. W. H. Russell, Alexander Majors and William B. Waddell often resulted in their contemporaries confusing the name of the firm involved in a particular operation.

Waddell and Russell were in the freighting business to California as early as 1854. When Russell organized the Leavenworth and Pikes Peak Express Company in February, 1859, Benjamin F. Ficklin appeared as a member of the firm—hardly a selection Russell would have made unless already well acquainted with the man.

Letters of Captain Jesse A. Gove, a member of the army expeditionary force to the Territory of Utah, definitely place him in the Fort Bridger-Salt Lake City area in 1858, when the wagons of Russell, Majors & Waddell, Army freighting contractors, were rolling to the embattled Mormon country. Gove refers to him variously as "express man" and "express rider."

During the late fall of 1857, Ficklin was employed as a deputy U. S. Marshal, *pro-tem*, for the Territory of Utah. Previously, he had joined the U. S. Wagon Road Survey party under W. M. F. Magraw. Magraw, it is recalled, held the mail contract between the Missouri River and Salt Lake City from 1854 to 1856. It is conceivable that Ficklin's employment in the survey party may have grown out of an earlier association with

Magraw on his mail line. The speculation on this tangent can go one step further. If that were true, then Ficklin would have been located along the route traveled by Senator Gwin in the fall of 1854.

Available evidence makes it fairly certain that he otherwise would have had little, if any, opportunity to meet Gwin until the first six months of 1860, when the Pony Express was inaugurated. During that time he visited Washington on company business. In the meantime, though, Gwin, as an influential member of the Senate Committee on Post Offices and Post Roads, was sure to have been sought out by, and to be quite familiar with, William H. Russell who, undisputedly, was the one who breathed life into the Pony idea. For long periods of time, he was an *habitué* of the nation's capitol, lobbying Congress and government officials for freight and mail contracts.

Those who hold the torch for him as conceiver of the horse express make a good and strong case out of the reference in Charles R. Morehead Jr.'s *Personal Recollections*. Morehead was an employee in charge of Majors & Russell's headquarters at Leavenworth City, two miles south of Fort Leavenworth. In the summer of 1857, when the company already had its wagon trains on the road to the West, it was required to organize additional trains to accompany the Army of Utah, marching from Fort Leavenworth to Salt Lake City. Morehead was pressed into service as assistant and clerk to the newly-hired Captain James Rupe, who was to lead the wagons. Rupe, an ex-soldier, conductor on the Santa Fe mail line and former wagonmaster, was the "most experienced plainsman then to be had," Morehead reported.

After excruciating hardship in delivering the freight that remained after Indian and Mormon raids, Rupe and Morehead returned to Fort Leavenworth on January 26, 1858. There they were summoned by a telegram from W. H. Russell to proceed to Washington. The big boss conducted them on a tour of the capital city, introducing the two frontiersmen to legislators and other government officials.

"With Mr. Floyd, Secretary of War," Morehead related, "the question of the feasibility of a pony express across the continent was presented by Mr. Russell, and fully discussed. Captain Rupe's views were called for, and he expressed the opinion that it was entirely practicable at all seasons on this route, all the way to California . . . While the Pony Express was conceived at that time by Mr. Russell, which was suggested to his mind by the success and circumstances of our trip in midwinter, 1,200 miles without change of animals in 30 days, it was not put into operation by him and his associates until 1860."

Although the statement stands almost unchallengeable on the counts of sincerity and clarity, researchers have lifted it out of the context of that portion of Morehead's *Recollections* dealing with Rupe.

The author went on to say that, while they were still in Washington, Russell tried to persuade Captain Rupe to return to the plains as general agent, but that the trainmaster declined, stating he had undergone enough hardship during and since the Mexican War and wished to return to his farm home and family. Subsequently, to Morehead, the Captain added:

"I do not wish to discourage you, but my advice is not to undertake the same kind of a trip again. Several times when I told you there was no danger [on their return trip eastward, alone] I had but little hope for our safety."

At this juncture the reader must draw his own interpretation of the conversation in Secretary Floyd's office. Obviously, Rupe's parting remark puts it in question.

How could the Captain counsel Morehead against taking "the same kind of a trip again," a journey on which *two* men traveled together, yet opine that the Pony Express would be entirely practicable in all seasons on the full distance of the route? Was the express that was so "fully discussed" the single-rider relay, or some other mode of mail transport? Morehead's reminiscences are nicely detailed and are happily free of the self-serving aspects so common to much other contemporary writing. His authorship, however, was dated about 40 years after the Pony expired, and in that span of time precise details are often fugitive.

Given the pregnant circumstances of the period, Russell's active mind, and his knack of welding chance and time into opportunity, it is reasonable to suppose that the horse relay suggestion reached him from several sources over a considerable period, and that he was the grand catalyst in bringing the idea into reality.

One of these sources seems to have been a group of his own employees. John Scudder, writing 29 years afterward, said that he and fellow workers of the company became interested in the overland mail controversy sweeping the country and calculated possible distances and time over the Central Route, on which the firm was then carrying coach mail in 1859. From Salt Lake City they addressed a letter to Russell which piqued his interest and brought a request for more details. Scudder recalls that they mapped their proposed route and recorded the necessity to build stations and provide for relays of mounted riders.

For some analysts Scudder's account may appear to be just a bit too pat. He goes on to add that nothing was heard following their exchange of correspondence with Russell until an order was received by A. B. Miller of Miller, Russell & Company, a merchandising enterprise established in Salt Lake City, to purchase 200 horses. Anyhow, unless the Scudder account is believed and the others not, it serves only as an addendum to the general subject, having been pre-dated by both the Rupe-Russell and Gwin-Ficklin stories.

More recently in the historical limelight than any of these candidates for the crown of inventive fame and honor is Frederick A. Bee, who, if but for the primacy of his self-interest in a fast overland mail, must be considered among the other reported originators of the idea. Colonel Bee (his title was acquired as provost marshal in northern California during the Civil War) was the founder, promoter and president of the first telegraph line to be strung eastward from the Golden State.

The names by which his company is referred to are almost as numerous as the sources of reference, but the Placerville, Humboldt & Salt Lake Telegraph Company is probably the original one. The first pole of the line was erected on July 4, 1858, and wire was strung along the main immigrant trail (frequently to trees) as far as Genoa, Nevada, by the fall of that year, and on to Carson City in the spring of 1859.

A more grandiose plan than to string a line simply to Salt Lake City apparently occurred to Bee, for the name "Placerville & St. Joseph Telegraph Co." is found in the record, as is "San Francisco and Overland Telegraph." He used the latter name himself when inserting a card in the *Alta California* on August 2, 1859, asking for "assistance in order to push the work forward." The transparent term "assistance" was a euphemism; Bee was looking for money.

Receiving little or none, he determined to ask Washington authorities for Federal aid. Before doing so, he is reported to have canvassed the proprietors of several San Francisco newspapers with a plan to establish a pony express from the Missouri River to the end of his telegraph line. Only the publishers of the *Alta*, Fredk. MacCrellish and William A. Woodward, are said to have seen merit in the proposal and agreed to back it to the tune of $12,000 a year "to have the news carried exclusively for their paper." Bee would have expected this support. MacCrellish was a member of his board of directors.

Accompanied by his brother, A. W. Bee, who was also interested in the company, Frederick traveled to Washington and,

U. S. Senator William M. Gwin of California, leader in the fight for adequate overland mail to the Pacific Coast. He was the political — but ineffective — friend of the Pony.

Frederick A. Bee, builder of the first telegraph line across the Sierras and strong advocate of the Pony Express.

The Pony Express rider as depicted for readers of the *Illustrated London News* in 1861. Curious feature is the saddlebag mail pouch instead of the *mochila*. The artist, G. H. Andrews, is said to have witnessed the arrival and departure of Pony riders at St. Joseph.

in the fall of 1859, "laid before the managers of Russell, Majors & Co. . . . a schedule showing that communication could be made between the end of his telegraph line and the Missouri River in 10 days." This was no amateur talking; as a Placerville horse dealer and stable keeper eight years earlier, he was well acquainted with horseflesh stamina. Then, with Russell, Bee is reported to have argued before the Senate Committee on Post Offices and Post Roads on "what could be done with a pony express running across country night and day, carrying the mails," the purpose being to win for Russell's company a daily mail service along the Central Route.

That attempt failed, but by February 19, 1860, the Washington correspondent of the San Francisco *Bulletin* was able to comment on the legislation authorizing the government to contract with several men, including F. A. Bee, for construction of an overland telegraph line, to be erected two years from July 31, 1860.

Before this Bee and Russell had gotten down to brass tacks on a split of revenue from telegrams which they would jointly carry. As narrated elsewhere in this volume, dispatches sent via the Pony were distinguished from letters by a separate set of charges. Russell had already announced the establishment of the express and had counted from the beginning on a tie-in with the telegraph companies. This was the very kind of cooperation envisioned by Bee. It meant that his tiny line in California could accept a telegram for New York, even though his wire stretched only to Carson City. Here was not merely "assistance" but a financial boon.

Parenthetically, MacCrellish's subsidy offer of $1,000 per month unquestionably was rejected out of hand, or withdrawn (if it really was made), because from the very start of the Pony Express newspapers generally in California printed eastern dispatches. Nonetheless, the *Alta* continued as a staunch moral supporter—and in a period of dire trial, a financial supporter—

of the express rider for as long as he streaked across mountain and plain with his *mochila* mail.

Whether one can conclude that Bee, urgently needing some such link like the Pony, gave birth to an original idea and first presented it to Russell, is fairly a matter of opinion. Pecuniary self-interest is a strong clue, but it is to be remembered that Russell, who never claimed the credit for himself, shared that incentive to even greater degree.

So, with all the facts, evidence, legend and supposition in and accounted for, the mystery is still a mystery. There is just one consolation. The idea, whose ever it was, produced a positive and bold action. Such was the terse wire that Russell sent to his son, John W., in Leavenworth:

HAVE DETERMINED TO ESTABLISH
A PONY EXPRESS TO SACRAMENTO,
CALIFORNIA. TIME TEN DAYS.

Chapter Three

THE FABULOUS WAGER

RUSSELL'S DECISION had all the earmarks of being a masterful stroke in strategy. Reaching it, he demonstrated a keen sense of timing and a rare insight into the trend of events.

Congress, ripped with dissension, failed miserably in getting agreement on adequate postal legislation during 1859. By adjournment, even the annual postal appropriation bill failed to pass. Considerably embarrassed, the department was obliged— when the President refused to convene a special session—to issue statements of indebtedness to contractors and agents. Some of these suffered losses when, up against it to pay bills of their own, they were forced to market the paper at a discount.

The death of the moderate Postmaster General Aaron V. Brown, in March, was a significant development. His administration had launched the Butterfield operation, as yet the only through mail transport overland from the Missouri River to the West. Enthusiastically, he had labeled it "a conclusive and triumphant success."

President Buchanan appointed the Kentuckian, Judge Joseph Holt, to fill the vacancy, and there was a remarkable about-face in policy. The post office department assumed a distinctly reactionary view toward anything connected with the overland mail. Sobered by the first year's meager $27,230 return in postal revenue over the Butterfield route, Holt caustically observed that, "Until a railroad shall have been constructed across the continent, the conveyance of the Pacific mails overland must be regarded as wholly impracticable."

Promptly, he embarked on a vigorous retrenchment program aimed at reducing his predecessor's operating loss of nearly $7,000,000. His indiscriminate axe-flaying, which hacked off substantial service along the struggling Central Route, ultimately reduced expenses by just under $90,000, or less than he realized from the cutback on the Chorpenning and Hockaday lines. He even attempted to raid the established Overland Mail line, but was held off by the Attorney General's interpretation of Butterfield's air-tight contract.

Through this maelstrom of congressional bickering and administrative ill-will, seemingly only W. H. Russell, the great opportunist, had a clear eye to the future. A month after Postmaster General Holt crippled Hockaday by his order to halve the service, Russell acquired the outfit, lock, stock and barrel. The deal was an entrepreneur's dream. Russell put up no cash, allowing Hockaday to keep the current quarter's contract payment, and gave the financially and physically ailing operator promissory notes totaling $120,250 for the balance.

Assuredly, the transport magnate must have had wind of, if not direct intelligence, that the same plight was in the offing for Chorpenning. For less than a month after the postal retrenchment axe had fallen on Hockaday, the California pioneer was notified his service and pay would be curtailed, effective July 1, 1859. It was a staggering blow. After safely, if roughly, delivering Horace Greeley to the Cary House in Placerville about the middle of July, the operation began to come apart at the seams. In a few months the sheriff started to sell off Chorpenning's stock to satisfy claims of creditors, and the following May the Post Office annulled his contract and advertised for bids. This was Russell's chance and he pounced, his tender winning the new contract for semimonthly service. He was to provide a 16-day schedule between Salt Lake City and Placerville, but the mails could be carried in any manner he saw fit.

Given these developments, a curious question now commands attention—why the Pony Express? If Russell had bagged the Hockaday contract and was soon to take over the Chorpenning route—a combination presenting him with through mail service from the Missouri River to California—why did he launch the courier mail? Was it, as averred in many historical accounts, to demonstrate the feasibility of the Central Route for year-around service?

Perhaps only partially so, and then as a means to an end. Mail had moved over the route since 1851, although, to be sure, in rather unreliable and irregular fashion. Popular opinion had it that the Central Route was largely a desert, unfit for settlement, inhabited by savages and subjected in winter to furious storms. Despite the completion of Captain James H. Simpson's topographical survey (unpublished until 1876) few facts were generally known of the country, particularly the arid land west of Salt Lake City.

More pointedly, the Pony Express is to be explained in terms of a gigantic gamble. At stake was a veritable monopoly in mail transport to California. Russell's unique plan, in effect, was a brave bet tossed in the poker game of postal policy.

Congress again in 1860 took up the overland mail question. From the outset it was clear that advocates of a broadened mail service wanted nothing less than a tri-weekly or daily service. Russell, aware of every move of the lawmakers, saw that any resulting contract would be in the proportion of a million dollars annual pay—a juicy plum.

The well-established Butterfield schedule was offering a semiweekly 23-day trip. Without a doubt, the shorter Central Route could better the time. What, then, could be a more practicable means of calling attention to that fact than the dramatic introduction of a service which sliced Butterfield's schedule in half? Of course, the proposed daily mail in coaches would not keep the fantastic speed of the Pony, but the publicity on the shorter distance would be valuable. A favorable opinion of the St. Joseph-Salt Lake-Sacramento route surely would result, and its present operators of the regular mail would be in an enviable position to bid for the new contract, if the law were passed.

As in the best laid plans of mice and men, that was the hitch. Congress bungled. So for another year, the Central Route would have to flounder along as a poor cousin of the postal service, leaving all the glory and most of the overland mail to Butterfield. The big bet was lost, for the time being.

Now any analysis of Russell's motive may fall short of hitting the precise mark, but the obvious circumstances surrounding the establishment of the Pony are difficult to ignore. In addition to the legislative aspects of the situation, the agile opportunist was caught in a Pandora's box of financial troubles that threatened a fatal sting. Accordingly, for the moment, the flying horse was a timely invention, stimulated by the hope of profit and gain. In that sense his incentive differed not one iota from the champions of commerce, before and after him.

Chapter Four

BLAZING THE TRAIL

T HE TELEGRAM to Leavenworth set off a frenzied activity in organizing the route, hiring people, building stations and accumulating tons of equipment and supplies. This was no time to dilly-dally if Russell's time table for an April 3rd inauguration of service was to be met. Benjamin F. Ficklin, in Washington at the time, immediately set out for the West where, the Washington *Evening Star* reported, he would set up "an independent horse express." He was one of the incorporators, as well as the route superintendent, of the Central Overland California & Pikes Peak Express Co., under whose auspices the Pony Express would run.

When Russell acquired the Hockaday line, he found the route without any stations whatever. Hockaday had simply stopped his stages every few hours and let his teams of four rest and graze. Russell decided to institute the relay system and built stations—or arranged for them at existing places along the road—at about 25-mile intervals. At the start the Pony's relays were arranged between the same stops, but soon, when it became evident that the speedy schedule required more frequent changes of horses, additional stations were provided so that fresh mounts were available every 10 or 12 miles.

Much of the land west of Salt Lake City, particularly beyond Ruby Valley, was a total emptiness and rarely afforded
convenient settlements or ranches. However, Chorpenning, in
his heyday, had spotted 14 stations along his route, and as this
was virtually to be followed by the Pony, they were easily
borrowed or appropriated. Others had to be built by crews sent
out from California and Utah.

While the operating sections of the line were being organized, connections were made in major cities to accumulate mail
for forwarding to the eastern terminus of the Pony Express at
St. Joseph, Missouri. Russell's own New York office was designated as the New York agency. In Washington, Chicago and
St. Louis other agency offices were established. At any of them
both businessmen and private individuals could deposit mail
for California and way points.

Under the almost impossible time limit set, it mattered little,
apparently, how entangled a later accounting would become
or what legal ramifications were involved in the methods used.
Get the job done—now! That was the urgent need.

Thus was the local-agent appointment of Samuel & Allen,
prominent Missouri commission merchants who kept offices at
132 North Second Street, St. Louis. John S. Jones signed them
up, acting as Russell's partner in Jones, Russell & Co. Why Jones,
who was the corporate secretary of the Central Overland, did
not make the appointment in that capacity, and what legal
effect it had, were questions that either did not bother the
Pony's proprietors or were left to the whims of chance.

Again, in Leavenworth, Jones, Russell & Co., not the operators
of the Pony Express, publicly advertised for "two hundred grey
mares, from four to seven years old, not to exceed fifteen hands
high, well broke to saddle, and warranted sound, with black
hooves, and suitable for running the overland Pony Express."
Out in Salt Lake City, 200 more horses were bought by

The main street of Placerville, as it looked in July, 1859, a few months before the Pony clattered through town with the first "flying" mail. Seated on the first coach with the white horses are Hank Monk, the famous stage "whip," and his renowned passenger, Horace Greeley.

Wells Fargo

A Pony Express rider (center, foreground) is pictured in this early wood engraving as having to dismount to let a pack train pass by on a narrow mountain pass.

Devil's Gate, a famous guidepost for westbound travelers on the overland immigrant trail, and a regular sight for Pony riders galloping along the Sweetwater River in what is now Wyoming. The landmark was passed some distance west of the Platte Bridge Station (present day Casper) and came into view near the Sweetwater Station. Photo was taken in 1859.
From the original in Library of Congress

Camp Floyd, Utah, Army headquarters during the Mormon conflict, as it appeared in 1859. In the following year it served as a relay point for the Pony Express. Copied from original in Library of Congress.

Exterior view of the walls of Fort Bridger, from an 1859 photograph. The Army sutler here, W. A. Carter, was appointed by Russell as Pony Express agent. From original in Library of Congress.

A. B. Miller. He may have been a part-time employee of the stage operation, but he primarily was there as a partner with Waddell and Russell in Miller, Russell & Co., vendors of general merchandise.

This seemingly haphazard manner of laying the groundwork did not, however, carry over to the actual selection of horses. Meticulous care was taken wherever they were bought, as not only the riders' lives but the promised speed of the express—its very success—would be dependent upon them. In California, the purchase of horses was entrusted to Maj. P. L. Solomon, U. S. Marshal at San Francisco. He was authorized to procure as fine a collection of fleet-footed and muscular quadrupeds as could be found. One hundred that he bought were of native California stock, small, wiry animals which already had turned in such an enviable record on the Butterfield stage route. He also purchased 29 mules to haul provisions for the stations to be established beyond the Sierras.

The total bill for putting horseflesh under saddle was in the neighborhood of $87,000. At a $175 average for 500 mounts the company paid what appears to have been a going market price, not for a hypothetical Pegasus or blooded race horse, but for a substantial, serviceable mount. Much emotional drivel and romantic foofuraw has been introduced into pulp-book history about the steed of the Pony rider, attributing to this rare animal supernatural speeds and endurance that have elevated him into a state of equine immortality.

Far from it. The giveaway is the Jones, Russell & Co. advertisement at Leavenworth, seeking horses "well broke and warranted sound"—not thoroughbred racers. It so happens that many of the horses purchased there were bought from Captain McKissack, quartermaster at Fort Leavenworth. Army service certainly was comparable—and a good recommendation—for the rough duty that was to be expected of a horse "suitable for running the overland Pony Express."

California's contribution could only have been of the same sturdy quality, differing perhaps in breed. With these, too, stamina was a more convincing qualification than speed. For 18 months these tough little horses had repeatedly been proving their worth to "whips", or drivers, of the Butterfield line. Twice a week they were pulling stages through the dreaded two-mile Apache Pass, east of Tucson, a natural, death-dealing Indian ambush where a high-strung, skittish thoroughbred would have been a frightful liability.

Interestingly, the Butterfield drivers discovered that the ponies of raiding Indians presented no competition, even to their teams of four or six, harnessed to a Concord. The Indian mustangs, they observed, were generally too poorly fed and cared for to match the endurance of the swift-wagon horses.

It is questionable whether in all the primitive western section of the United States, in the territories, there were as many as 500 blooded horses, much less 500 for sale. But horses in the price range paid by the Pony Express were available, and the going cost is verified by the record of another, proposed large lot purchase. In the fall of 1857, Captain Jno. H. Dickerson, assistant quartermaster of Camp Scott, stationed at Fort Bridger, filed a proposal to buy 400 horses and 800 mules in the New Mexico area. He carefully detailed the costs, allowing $26,250 to purchase 150 "American horses," or $175 each for the lot.

Judging from the time allowed to secure them, horses were at a greater premium than riders, because herds of horses were already in corrals at both ends of the line before riders were signed up. At the western terminus adventuresome lads weren't hired until 72 hours before departing to take their places along the route.

All told, how many daring souls volunteered for the rugged and lonely saddle life has long been one of the better hidden secrets of the Pony. Latter-day admirers have been obliged to observe a sort of writers' roulette game in which various authorities have plumped down on the numbers 50, 60 and 80. But, unfortunately, the little white ball keeps bouncing. By close attention to detail, let's see if a more accurate conjecture than a spread of 30 numbers can be arrived at. There are two clues to follow and some schoolboy arithmetic to solve.

First, there is a tiny advertisement in the pages of the Sacramento *Union* for March 19, 1860, here gladly given its first additional circulation:

> MEN WANTED! The undersigned wishes to hire ten or a dozen men, familiar with the management of horses, as hostlers, or riders on the Overland Express Route via Salt Lake City. Wages $50 per month and found. I may be found at the St. George Hotel during Sunday, Monday and Tuesday.
>
> WILLIAM W. FINNEY

Newspaper readership in those days, without the harassing distractions of myriad forms of entertainment, must have been thorough, indeed. About 200 pairs of eyes were attracted to Finney's few lines of small type, buried deep in a maze of general advertising. That many eager young hopefuls called at the St. George Hotel and must have fairly swamped the prospective employer. One thing is assured, they were duly impressed. Finney's selection of a "hiring hall" showed good, if expensive taste. The St. George was reputed a "very fine one, the best in the state . . . as nice as any hotel in New York." By the afternoon of the second day an inquiring *Union* reporter was able to write in the news columns that "the requisite number of post-riders on the Overland Express had been engaged."

Clue No. 2 is the oft-quoted announcement of Finney's departure from Sacramento with his 129 head of livestock and "21 men as express riders and packers," together with tents and supplies, to establish stations as far east as Eagle Valley." That destination was patently an erroneous report, as Eagle Valley lay at the foot of the eastern slope of the Sierras and was reached by a relay of only two riders; and in the intervening distance stations were arranged for at established roadside inns, making the assignment of station keepers unnecessary. In confusing contradiction, the announcement added that he would travel on to Ruby Valley "to fix upon the points for the stations and make a proper distribution of men and horses." There he would have trekked about two-thirds the way to Salt Lake City, perhaps 500 miles as the trail was found.

Exactly how many of the express riders and packers announced as accompanying him to stock the stations were finally picked for the saddle is still a mystery. But a fairly accurate estimate can be hit upon by easy computation. On leaving Sacramento, Finney's reported intention was to fix stations at a distance of 20 to 25 miles, so that each horse would travel from one to another station twice a week. An expressman was to travel 35 to 75 miles, changing horses at each relay point, using three horses for a one-way trip.

If we calculate from the minimum trip distance of 35 miles for a rider, we will determine the maximum number of riders that could have been hired by the western boss. Fourteen of them, at that rate, would put the mail 490 miles from Sacramento. Now, projecting this minimum rider distance as actual over the 1,966-mile route between Sacramento and St. Joseph, the requirement is found to be not more than 56 expressmen.

More likely, there would have been fewer, because contemporary accounts generally describe a rider's regular stint as ranging from 75 to 100-odd miles. Furthermore, the Central Overland California & Pikes Peak Express Co. was at the very start feeling a financial pinch and, to meet higher than anticipated expenses, had borrowed from Ben H. Holladay, then in San Francisco. In this circumstance, it's difficult to suppose the company would have generously provided the route with idle or surplus help.

Putting aside the puzzle on their number, one can easily become enchanted with another conundrum—their motives. To the young men tied to the occasional farms homesteaded along the route in the middle and eastern divisions perhaps the romance of the racing mail offered a happy release from the humdrum life of milking cows, feeding chickens and tilling the land. But what was it in the teeming cities of St. Jo and Sacramento, the very hub of life, where there was the excitement of a railroad, a river levee crowded with strange ships, and all the tempestuous living in a booming town? Out west, surely it couldn't have been Finney's unglamorous offer of $50 a month and found; double that could have been earned in the fabulous Washoe Mines, had a lad but the will to scale the Sierras and get to Carson City. Possibly there is no answer, except youth itself and youth's flight from adolescence and an urge to risk the unknown.

Whether farm boy or city lad, the applicant found a fairly standardized set of qualifications to meet. These, it is supposed, were established by Alexander Majors and Ben Ficklin, both of whom were men of wide experience on the frontier, personally familiar with much of the rugged route. Their word on how much of a daily strain man and horse should endure would tend to prevail. So, whether a rider was assigned to dash across the Kansas prairie, or trace the Platte River, or plunge through the barren Utah wasteland, with few exceptions, he was apt to be poured from the same mold.

Typically, he was slight in build, wiry in strength, sound of limb and mind, and about 18 to 20 years of age. He was, of course, an accomplished, fearless horseman, a requirement easy to come by in the broad, uncharted West where boys grew into manhood virtually on horseback.

Legend and fact often defy distinction in much of the grand saga of the Pony Express, but this much is fairly affirmed: of this band of tough, brave, keen express riders, few cringed or faltered along the way. Many kept to the saddle even when payless pay days had come and gone. Most of them gallantly rode headlong over mountains of loneliness, some down the path of bloodied death, but all into the infinity of proud glory.

Equipage for man and horse concerned the express managers as much as the selection of riders. Weight was of prime importance. The speedy 10-day transit was crucially dependent upon the lightness of load. Hence, the ordinary western saddle was considered too heavy, and often substituted for it was a modified *vaquero* model with a trimmed "skirt", a low, sloping cantle and a broad, short horn. Light wooden stirrups sometimes had protective *tapaderas* to fend off brush from the rider's legs. All told, the complete product had but a third the heft of the western equivalent regularly in use.

Several suppliers are said to have furnished these special saddles, among them being Israel Landis of St. Joseph, Missouri. Some were reported to have been purchased by General Agent Finney in Sacramento or San Francisco for equipping the western division.

Over the entire equine seat there was placed a well-tailored leather vest—the storied *mochila*. This was the mail bag of the expressman, his *raison d'être*. As with all the rider's other accoutrements, it was designed for speed. Made of a tough, well-tanned hide about one-eighth inch thick, there were securely sewn to it four stiff leather *cantinas*—boxes—to carry the mail. Two were on each side, fore and aft of the rider's thigh. Openings in the center, or top, of the *mochila* let it fit firmly and snugly over the horn and cantle, forming a sort of covering blanket for the saddle.

The rider, galloping into a remount station, had only to jerk free his *mochila,* throw it on an already saddled fresh horse held waiting, and he was away again. It is said that the four *cantinas* were secured with brass locks, but way stations had access to one of them in which was placed a waybill for recording times of arrival and departure along the route. Once the waybill had a more urgent purpose, when the Salt Lake City agent hastily scribbled on it the startling news that Indians had chased all the men from eastern Nevada stations and that the *mochila* had been lost.

Neither time nor money permitted, at the outset, the complete outfitting of the line with these singular mail-toting saddle covers, and early drawings of danger-daring post riders pictured them astride galloping horses equipped with a pair of conventional saddlebags. In the opinion of one observer the standard pouches might as well have contained hardtack and biscuits, for all the prudence taken in their handling. He noted that the leathern bags "are thrown about carelessly enough when the saddle is changed," with little regard for the contents.

Curiously, much of the weight saved in saddlery was, in the beginning, lost in armament. At this time Pony riders were bristling with weapons, wearing two revolvers, a bowie-knife and carrying a rifle. That was more artillery than provided the armed stagecoach messengers whose cargo of passengers and gold was far more valuable than the few pounds of oilskin-wrapped letters charged to the Pony.

The revolvers of the express rider traditionally have been identified as Navy Colts, which would have been of the 1851 model, then in popular use. This huge pistol was a five-shot, percussion fired, .36-caliber weapon, with an octagonal-shaped barrel, the loading lever omitted. It was not an automatic, but had to be cocked for each firing. Some question is admissible on its reported general use, due to the pistol's ponderous weight.

A more plausible gun would have been the Wells Fargo model Colt, a short pocket pistol made mainly with a three-inch, octagonal-shaped barrel. Like the Navy Colt, it was percussion fired and a five-shot revolver, but used a lighter, .31-caliber ball. Some 200,000 guns of this model had been manufactured and were available by 1860, and their use by stagecoach messengers would tend to suggest their adoption by the Pony Express. Although not so powerful a weapon as the Navy Colt, it has been recorded that express riders, when under threat of attack, were urged to resort to speed, "to run rather than fight," and so the lighter gun would seem to have filled the need just as well.

Practically speaking, a number of different types were seen along the trail. Original equipment was purchased at both ends of the line and identical firearms in quantity could not have been expected from the widely separated suppliers. Early in the Pony's life the Army near Salt Lake City furnished guns for protection against marauding Indians, and at about the same time Finney, at Carson City, asked for the loan of 20 dragoon pistols.

The Spencer rifle, despite repeated reference to it in Pony Express annals, was not carried. It was an extremely heavy gun, made by the Spencer Repeating Rifle Company of Boston. A seven-shot repeater, it was tremendously powerful, firing a .56-caliber cartridge. George Repaire, an eminent modern authority on old guns, was good enough to point out to the author that the Spencer was not patented until March 6, 1860, less than a month prior to the Pony's inaugural service, and that the "bugs" in its novel repeating mechanism, having subsequently given the manufacturer annoying trouble, delayed its general use until nearly the close of the Civil War, when it was used by Yankee forces in the South.

In any event, two revolvers, a rifle, a knife, plus a horn to sound his coming, proved too much luggage for the express rider to tote (and possibly too costly for his employers to supply), so most of it was discarded for the greater part of the Pony's existence. Finally settled upon was a single pistol, with an extra loaded cylinder occasionally carried.

Ignoring his detractors, one can only admire the organizational genius of William H. Russell, tycoon of western trans-

St. Joseph in 1861, as seen from the Kansas side of the Missouri River. From the *Illustrated London News.*

Rock Creek, Nebraska, Pony Express and Overland Stage station where three men were gunned down by "Wild Bill" Hickok in 1861. Man on horse holding a bottle has been identified as David McCanles, station agent, and one of those killed. From an original daguerreotype.

PONY EXPRESS.

NINE DAYS FROM SAN FRANCISCO

To New York.

THE CENTRAL OVERLAND PONY EXPRESS CO. will start their LETTER EXPRESS from San Francisco to New York and intermediate points,

On Tuesday, the 3d day of April next,

And upon every TUESDAY thereafter, at 4 o'clock, P. M.

Letters will be received at San Francisco until 3¾ o'clock, P. M., each day of departure.

OFFICE—**Alta Telegraph Office,** Montgomery street

Telegraphic Dispatches will be received at Carson City until 6 o'clock, P. M., every Wednesday.

Schedule Time from San Francisco to New York:

For Telegraphic Dispatches, 9 days;

For Letters, 13 days.

Letters will be charged between San Francisco and Salt Lake City, $3 per half ounce and under, and at that rate according to weight. To all points BEYOND Salt Lake City, $5 per half ounce and under, and that rate according to weight.

Telegraphic Dispatches will be subject to the same charges as Letters.

All Letters must be enclosed in stamped Envelopes.

WM. W. FINNEY,

mh17-tf Agent Central Overland Pony Express Co.

Times copy.

Wells Fargo

The beginning and end of the Pony Express. At left is the first advertisement to appear anywhere, as reproduced from the San Francisco *Evening Bulletin* of March 17, 1860. In the succinct announcement below (*Bulletin,* October 26, 1861), Wells, Fargo & Co. writes *finis* to the short career of the gallant Pony. This word however, proved a bit hasty.

Bancroft Library

NOTICE.

BY ORDERS FROM THE EAST,

THE PONY EXPRESS

WILL be DISCONTINUED.

The Last Pony coming this way left Atchinson, Kansas, yesterday.

oc25-1t **WELLS, FARGO & CO., Agents.**

Johnny Fry, Pony Express rider out of St. Joseph, Missouri, often credited with making the initial ride on April 3, 1860. He was a Federal scout in the Civil War and was killed in battle.

port. After absorbing the Hockaday line into the Leavenworth & Pikes Peak Express Company, staggering expenses inside of six months nearly forced the line to the wall. Before acquiring Hockaday it operated primarily as a passenger service between Leavenworth and the rich mines at Denver, on any schedule that paying patrons made possible. It was an enterprise started by Russell and John S. Jones, an overland freighter, in February, 1859. Now, with debts of over a half-million, the firm of Russell, Majors & Waddell took it over as a matter of self-protection against Russell's speculation. At the outset Waddell and Majors wanted nothing to do with the line and now they were its unwilling owners. In November, 1859, it was reorganized as the Central Overland California & Pikes Peak Express Company and new stock was sold. Russell emerged on top as president. It was a neat—if necessary—contortion in refinancing.

With the turn of the year he proceeded to demonstrate an equal adeptness in laying out the organization for the Pony Express. Compared to his massive freighting enterprises, the effort required little capital. It was perceived that, wherever possible, arranging of rider relay points at existing farm houses and wayside inns would be easier and less costly than constructing company stations; and doing so would frequently save the wage cost of company employees who otherwise would have to be sent out as keepers and stock tenders.

Something of this reasoning was likewise followed in detailing the management of the route. Just as the horses were bought at Leavenworth and Salt Lake City by associates rather than employees, so could the present superintendents along the stage line double up their work and supervise the upcoming express operation. Between the Missouri River and Salt Lake there were three of them, counting Slade and Bromley, who had carried over to Russell's regime from Hockaday. Beyond the Mormon town two had to be hired.

A. E. Lewis managed the line from St. Joseph to Fort Kearny. At that point the superintendency of the notorious Captain Jack (Joseph A.) Slade, experienced murderer and whiskey drinker, took over, extending beyond Fort Laramie to Horseshoe Station. From there to Salt Lake the route was in charge of James E. Bromley. He kept his headquarters at Weber Station, several relay points east of Salt Lake. The next division west was under Major Howard Egan, one of Brigham Young's personal bodyguards during the leader's hegira from Nauvoo, Illinois, and a trail blazing cattle drover to California. His superintendency ran to Roberts Creek Station, in the middle of the mountain-serrated desert. Thence, to the foot of the Sierras, the route came under the jurisdiction of Bolivar Roberts, who headquartered at Carson City.

William W. Finney, who carried the magnificent title of General Agent of the Pacific, managed the operation over the Sierras into Sacramento, and represented the company's interests in San Francisco. His broader duties placed him a cut above a route superintendent. Some writers have placed Bolivar Roberts' management westward over the mountains as far as Sacramento, but contemporary events show that the active bossing in that area was the responsibility of Finney and later his successor.

All the difficulties and emergencies stemming from the ravages of man and nature along the gossamer trail, stretching thinly across a virtual no man's land, were heaped on the shoulders of these six men. Any one of them, by the circumstances of his situation, had to be a stronger, tougher, more resourceful man than those he hired. Indeed, like Howard Egan, he had to be ready not merely to manage and control, but temporarily to substitute for a rider whenever the necessity required.

He had to contrive to watch the condition of livestock and to supervise their care, and in emergencies provide additional horses when none were to be had. He was responsible for find-

ing and hiring experienced riders to substitute for the sick or
lame, or to take the places of those who quit the saddle. When
stations were attacked and burned, and their keepers massacred
by the Indians, his was the task of repairing and restaffing the
broken link.

Overlying all these demands was still his basic job, the
stage line and its separate problems, not helped in the least by
the frequent complaints of uncomfortable, hungry and exasper-
ated passengers. It was perhaps in the natural sequence of
things that his overall authority tended to give him an ex-officio
status as constable and magistrate over the people and territory
he ruled, and if his administration of justice, like the crude Captain Jack Slade's, could not always be fair, at least it was swift.

As the physical organization of the line began to shape into
a semblance of order, promotional preparations were made for
the development of business. Mostly, these efforts were limited to advertising in the various newspapers, the only medium
of the time for communicating to the mass public. In keeping
with the mode of the day, Pony Express advertisements were
phrased in plain, man-of-the-street, charmless prose, hardly dis-
tinguishable from the unexciting announcement of a new ship-
ment of baled cordage or black iron shovels.

Yet, a more than cursory glance at these history-making
ads rewards the reader with intelligence he otherwise might
overlook. For instance, the ads show that the St. Joseph terminus, *per se*, was relatively unimportant and rarely mentioned.
Neither was the actual 10-day transit time of the Pony.

More vital in the eyes of the express' proprietors was a large
flow of letters between the eastern metropolitan centers and the
western end of the line. Hence, the lapsed time for communications between New York and San Francisco was the ads'
prominent feature.

Incidentally, an interesting *faux pas* apparently was made in
calculating the time element for the first ad to appear in the

east, which was signed by no less a personage than W. H. Russell himself. Printed in the New York *Herald* and the St. Louis *Missouri Republican,* the announcement promised that telegraph messages would be delivered in San Francisco in eight days. Out in San Francisco the *Evening Bulletin* ad of March 17, 1860—the Pony's first paid advertisement anywhere—gave the time as nine days. Subsequently, this was reduced to eight, then soon corrected again to nine days. Correspondingly, the early promise of 12-day delivery on letters between New York and San Francisco was rescinded in favor of 13 days.

The whole story of this advertising presents a strange paradox. The Pony Express, bravely, even foolishly, launched without government subsidy or the firm promise of one, itself gave a handsome subsidy to the telegraph lines. A San Francisco letter writer had to pay, the early ads advised, "$3 per half ounce or under and at that rate according to weight" for delivery in Salt Lake City. Beyond Salt Lake the rate was five dollars (which later prevailed regardless of destination). But telegraph dispatches, stuffed with letters in the same *mochila,* rode between the Carson City and St. Joseph telegraph terminals at less than half the letter rate—just two dollars and 45 cents.

True, as the distance between the ends of the wire narrowed, the shorter would become the carriage of messages. Without the express, however, the telegraph would have been stymied for overland traffic until it had been completely built. Or, had Russell not chosen to cooperate with the wire promoters, dispatches would have had to go as letters at the regular and higher mail rate.

But cooperate he did, and details of the agreement were made public with the first Pony Express mail to arrive in California from the East.

Ten words from any Atlantic city or vice versa $2.45
Ten words between any two California stations
(telegraph) 2.00

Expressing message without regard to length between
    eastern and western telegraph terminals. 2.45
Each additional word for the entire distance. 20

Most Pony Express advertising—some of which detailed the
above charges—gave equal emphasis to both telegraph dispatches and regular express mail. In California much was
made of the fact that a dispatch could be wired to Carson City
27½ hours later than the closing of the Pony mail in San Francisco; it took that long for the express to reach the end of
Frederick Bee's "grapvine." Normally, these dispatches, on arrival at St. Joseph, were handed over to the office of the eastern
telegraph line for re-sending to the addressee; but if the sender
elected to have them deposited there in the U. S. Post Office,
he was charged the regular letter mail rate for the intermediate
Pony service, rather than the lower telegraph rate.

In the early stages of getting the express ready to run, another effort of the proprietors to develop business was hinted
at. Someone—surely it was Russell—planted the idea with the
British Minister in Washington that the fast horse mail could
be of especial service to His Majesty's government in transmitting official papers.

Reportedly, the Englishman was impressed and "expressed
some decided opinions concerning this fast channel of communication across the continent. He gives it his hearty support, and
pledges the same from his government, so soon as he lays before
it the details of the advantages to British commerce to ensue
from it, which he proposes doing by the next Liverpool mail."

Evidently the Minister's suggestion was well taken, for W.
F. Bailey, writing 38 years later, states that the English government became one of the principal patrons of the Pony
Express, and that, in one instance, a report of the operations of
an English squadron in China waters required $135 to cover
express charges.

Chapter Five

IN THE SADDLE

AT LAST THE DAY had arrived. This was the grand moment when two doughty riders—one at each end of the line—would leap astride impatient horses and dash away through a curtain of legend, which ever since has masked their trail with confusion and mystery. No part of the Pony Express story seems larded with quite so much conjecture, pure opinion and doubt as the stirring event of this first crossing with the mail.

The enigma begins at St. Joseph. In all the huzzas and hurly-burly that accompanied the send-off, no one apparently thought to record for posterity exactly the place in the city where the grand race began, or the identity of the expressman who had the distinguished honor of carrying the initial *mochila*.

Alex Carlisle, Charles Cliff, Gus Cliff, Johnny Fry, Jack H. Keetley, William Richardson and Henry Wallace—seven riders in all—have been named as the lad in the saddle of the bright bay mare (or the little sorrel, or the jet-black horse—take your choice), said to be named Sylph, which galloped out of town at 7:15 p.m., April 3, 1860. His identification, not quite settled a century later, has been sifted down by process of literary attrition to a draw between Johnny Fry and William Richardson. The patient reader may study the arguments of their respective advocates, ably presented in various publications and books, then decide for himself, perhaps with the aid of a flipped coin.

Fry or Richardson, he was delayed two hours and 15 minutes beyond the departure time promised by Russell in his advertising. A special messenger, riding a train from the east with Pony Express mail deposited in the big city off-line agencies, had missed his connection at Detroit. Word of the emergency was flashed to George H. Davis, roadmaster of the new Hannibal & St. Joseph Railroad, at Hannibal, Missouri.

Until now the rail line had not been favored with a government postal contract, the mail for St. Joseph being hauled up river by boat. Here was the big chance to prove the railroad's worth to Uncle Sam. At St. Joseph a special train had been made up for the occasion and dispatched 160 miles east to await the messenger.

Davis ordered all trains off the main line and every switch spiked. He selected Ad Clark, a "nervy, fearless engineer," to make the run at the throttle. His train consisted of the wood-burner engine *Missouri,* with tender and one car.

Fuel agents between Hannibal and St. Joseph were instructed to stand by for loading the tender "in less than no time." Engineer Clark received instructions equally terse: make a speed record that would last 50 years!

When the messenger arrived at Hannibal from Detroit and climbed aboard with several other passengers, the little train took off in a cloud of steam and smoke. The first 70 miles was over fairly straight and level roadbed, and here Ad Clark's speed was estimated at a frightening 60 miles per hour. Then came Macon, and C. S. Coleman's fuel stop. On the platform men were waiting with armloads of wood. In just 15 seconds the tender was replenished and the train jerked down the track, rapidly gaining speed. The passengers gripped their seats as the car crazily rocked sideways, threatening to dump them on the floor.

Ahead was the steep grade down to the Chariton River. Ad Clark took it "like an avalanche," a hot blast of fire shooting out the stack and wood sparks streaming backwards like crimson snowflakes. Nobody aboard was aware that he eased off the throttle. He probably didn't; no other engineer in the employ of the railway ever equalled his time over that section of the road.

A few minutes past 7:00 p.m., the little train pulled into the St. Joseph depot. Clark "stepped majestically from his iron horse, looking mussed up, grimy and grand." Unbelievably, he had made the long run in only four hours and 51 minutes. For the instant, he was the hero, the Pony Express almost forgotten.

Even though his errand was the very reason for Clark's hair-raising run, somehow no one learned the messenger's name. He simply turned his mail pouch over to company officials and then evaporated from the scene forever. The contents were transferred to a waiting *mochila* by Joseph S. Roberson, a station employee, a cannon at the Patee House boomed a salute and the rider (Richardson or Fry?) was ready to fly to the river, where the ferry *Denver* would carry him to the opposite shore.

Russell, Alexander Majors and Mayor M. Jeff Thompson had made a point of attending the departure, and their presence—despite the delay—lent the affair a proper sense of dignity and aplomb. Sometime between five o'clock and 7:15 p.m. solemn speeches were profoundly delivered, one by Majors, another by Mayor Thompson, both of whom turned prophets to declare the Pony was the harbinger of the Pacific railroad. Russell apparently did not speak, or if he did, his words were not recorded.

Neither, at least with accuracy, was the number of letters which the rider sped westward. Supposedly, he carried 49 letters, five telegrams and a few special editions of eastern newspapers, printed on special lightweight paper. On arrival at Sacramento, though, the *Union* reported that rider Hamilton had brought about 80 letters for this city and San Francisco. It is doubtful that the scant volume of mail from way stations would have accounted for the discrepancy.

During the preceding days' preparations William H. Russell may have been the cause of a broken promise concerning the forwarding of newspapers by the first rider. Notwithstanding the fact that his *mochila* contained special editions of the New York *Herald* and *Tribune,* likely by his invitation, the St. Joseph *Gazette* felt that it, alone, would have this honor, and in a heavily leaded account of the new enterprise, said:

"Through the politeness of the express company we are permitted to forward by the first pony express the first and only newspaper which goes out, and which will be the first newspaper ever transmitted to California in eight days. The first pony will start precisely at five o'clock this afternoon . . ."

Any such misunderstanding was of no concern to the rider. He spurred out of the crowd of well-wishers, toward the river and the waiting ferry, which had been alerted by the boom of the cannon. All along the route relief riders were expecting that he had already started and was by now halfway to Granada, the first "home" station. There was, for this expressman, over two hours of precious time to be made up.

The assembled populace, "all St. Joe, great and small," was cheated by the after-dark departure from appreciating the full effect of the flamboyant costume he wore. Elsewhere on the route riders dressed as they pleased, but at St. Joseph Russell's propensity for showmanship dictated a different policy. According to a letter written by Pony rider J. H. Keetley, quoted by Wm. L. Visscher, the lads at the eastern terminus "always rode out of town with silver mounted trappings decorating both man and horse and regular uniforms with plated horn, pistol, scabbard, and belt, etc., and gay flower-worked leggings and plated jingling spurs resembling, for all the world, a fantastic circus rider." He remembered that, once on the ferry, the rider was provided a room in which to shed this festive adornment and dress himself in more serviceable clothing. So the American public's fancy had been humored; now there was work ahead.

Five days and 23 hours later there still was hard work ahead and lost time to regain. At 6:30 p.m., April 9th, the flying *mochila* had reached Salt Lake City. By now the two-hour tardiness at St. Joseph had stretched beyond a full day. The schedule had specified that the mail would be here in 124 hours, or by 9 p.m. the previous evening. It began to look like the 10-day service was a figment of Russell's imagination.

Quickly, the mail pouch was flung over a fresh horse and a new rider sped away westward. From here on, some exceptional riding across the mountain-broken vastness of the western Utah Territory and over the precipitous Sierras would have to take place if any semblance of schedule were to be preserved.

At San Francisco the ceremony for the send-off of the first eastbound rider was purely for publicity and propaganda purposes, as it was planned that Sacramento, not the Golden Gate city, was to be the operating terminus of the route. So for first-rate entertainment it suffered in comparison to the departure at St. Joseph, lacking the breathlessness of a tardy train-borne messenger, and the impressiveness of speeches by the express' promoters. Like a signboard, "a clean-limbed hardy little nankeen-colored pony," his harness bedecked with miniature flags, was tethered at the door of the Alta Telegraph Company's office on Montgomery Street, from one o'clock until departure time, set for a few minutes before four p.m.

There being no riders stationed in San Francisco, a chap named James Randall posed as expressman, and mounted the brownish-yellow horse—from the wrong side. The mail was on its way, amid shouts from a group of curious idlers. In Randall's *mochila* were 56 letters, which, at the five dollar per half-ounce rate, brought a receipt of $280.

No other rider was ever recorded as having such a short tour of duty, for he galloped only a few blocks to the waterfront and to the waiting river steamer, *New World*. Historians generally agree that the express career of this rider-by-proxy ended here, and that the mail was carried in the boat, unaccompanied, to Sacramento.

Nearly 10 hours later, at 2:40 a.m. next morning, the vessel tied up to the Sacramento levee. At this point, until recent years, confusion over the next riders' identities was like St. Joseph all over again. Various writers, including no less an authority than Alexander Majors himself, writing when an elderly man, have named Harry Roff to be the first lad eastbound out of Sacramento. At Placerville "Boston" was said to have taken over, surrendering the mail at Friday's Station to Sam Hamilton, who carried it through to Fort Churchill beyond Carson City.

Contemporary newspapers, however, have revealed that the 144 miles between Sacramento and Carson City were covered by only two riders, whose trail we shall follow.

In just five minutes after the *Antelope* had arrived, William Hamilton, now unquestionably identified, had the *mochila* over his saddle, and was off for the mountains with no more fanfare than perhaps a wave and a "good luck" from the Alta Telegraph agent. For the rest of the town, the early hour was no enticement for a gay celebration. Added to his cargo of correspondence were 13 letters from Sacramento writers, a quantity that so disgraced the city's support of the Pony that the *Union* was a week in admitting it.

Hamilton's route was via the White Rock road, stopping at the Five Mile House, Fifteen Mile House and Mormon Tavern for changes of horses. The road, well marked by heavy stage and wagon traffic, took him by Mud Springs (El Dorado), Diamond Springs and into Placerville. He arrived there at 6:40

a.m., covering the 45 miles from Sacramento in three hours and 45 minutes. Moments later, at 6:48 a.m., he was in the saddle of a fresh horse, held for him at the office of the Alta Telegraph on the town plaza opposite the post office, and on his way over the mountains, flying. Another hour and 12 more miles, Hamilton reached Sportsman Hall where he found Warren Upson ready and waiting to carry on.

For sheer physical hardship, Upson's ride was to be a monument to determination and skillful horsemanship. A heavy blizzard had blown up and was to continue throughout the day. Heading upward toward the summit, his ride became a white nightmare in which Upson alternately rode and walked, leading his horse over the trail where wagon marks had disappeared and landmarks were blotted out in the swirling snow.

It was the first time in three years that all stage line travel had become stalled both ways from the summit. The busy traffic between the Washoe Mines and Sacramento had come to a standstill, but Upson doggedly fought his way on. He found fresh horses posted at established relay stations, and finally reached Hope Valley where he turned off for Woodford's on the sharp decline of the trail down to Genoa. A last change of horses here, and he was on the final leg of his run to Carson City. Two days afterward the Sacramento *Union* reported the storm was still continuing and that there was no feed on the road, except that held by the stage lines and the Pony Express, "who won't sell at any price." By the seventh of April some wagon trains, which had attempted the ascent, were forced back to Placerville.

There is likely no more detailed and graphic description of the devastated and hazardous conditions existing along this main immigrant thoroughfare than that written by J. Ross Browne, who, afoot, negotiated the entire trail to Carson City, over the very route taken by Upson, only a few days after the latter's epic ride.

"The road from Placerville to Strawberry Flat is for the most part graded, and no doubt is a very good road in summer; but it would be a violation of conscience to recommend it in the month of April," Brown noted.

"In many places it seemed absolutely impracticable for wheeled vehicles . . . for the road was literally lined with broken-down stages, wagons, and carts, presenting every variety of aspect, from the general smash-up to the ordinary capsize. Wheels had taken rectangular cuts to the bottom; broken tongues projected from the mud; loads of dry goods and whiskey-barrels lay wallowing in the general wreck of matter . . . whole trains of pack mules struggled frantically to make the transit from one dry point to another; burros . . . frequently were buried up to the neck . . . Now and then an enterprising mule would emerge from the mud, and, by attempting to keep the edge of the road, lose his foothold, and go rolling to the bottom of the canyon, pack and all."

Reaching Strawberry, Browne was amazed to find several hundred men stranded at this "best stopping place and last station before crossing the summit of the Sierra Nevada." There already were some 250 tired wayfarers snoring in double-shotted bunks in the upstairs "bedroom," so the landlord provided him with a layout, i.e., sleeping space on the floor of a small parlour, where he could use his own blankets for bed and covering.

The next morning, standing at the front door, he was dismayed to find the place covered with two or three feet of snow, and more falling steadily in dark and threatening weather. But he determined to press on. Two miles away, the road, or what was left of it, was cluttered with pack trains that had broken through the old snow in many places, leaving deep holes only partially hidden by the new snow. Browne gingerly sought a way around these "regular man-traps."

Short cuts across the trail were tempting but, he found, fraught with danger. Trying one, "some trifling obstruction deprived me of the use of my feet at the very start, after which I traveled down in a series of gyrations at once picturesque and

complicated. When I reached the bottom, I was entirely unable
to comprehend how it had all happened; but there I was, pack
and baggage, all safely delivered in the snow—bones sound and
free of expense."

Finally, at Woodford's, the last station on the way over to
Carson Valley and Genoa, J. Ross Browne found the snow
"pretty well gone from the canyon"—a relieving and welcome
sight for both him and his predecessor, the intrepid Warren
Upson, who, unlike the foot traveler, had forced his way over
the same storm-torn trail without benefit of rest.

Carson City was the end of Upson's spectacular ride. His
speed against the heavy odds of nature brought favorable comment in the California press in only a day or so after he reined
up at the Pony's office in the little community. It bragged a
population of some 1,200 souls, mostly transient, and was the
jumping off point for the great void that spanned the distance
to Salt Lake City. Across this desert vacuum there were no
newspapers or telegraph keys to record the Pony's passing,
and the names of the riders who relayed the mail eastward from
the tiny hamlet remains another unsolved mystery.

Latterly written accounts that have listed expressmen by
name disconcertingly fail to agree. Two such records, however,
identify Howard Egan, the division superintendent between
Salt Lake City and Roberts Creek, as the rider who brought
the *mochila* into the Mormon capital.

There, on arrival of the Pony Express, the *Deseret News*,
an enthusiastic supporter ("although the telegraph is very desir-
able, we feel well satisfied with this achievement for the present"), proudly said that the mail had come inside of prospectus
time. Based on the published westward schedule, the Pony's
hooves were to have clattered through Salt Lake City and up to
the State Street office of the company in 119 hours out of San
Francisco, the advertised western end of the route and starting

point of the trip. Actually, the mail arrived at 11:45 p.m., April 7th, after only 104 hours on the road. The last 75 miles were made in only five hours and 15 minutes, rider and horse sloshing over a heavily mudded road in stormy spring weather.

East of Salt Lake City the storm retarded the Pony's progress and the next rider took five hours to reach Snyder's Mill, 25 miles distant. But as more miles were clipped off, and relay after relay was made, the road conditions improved. Horses were changed at Fort Bridger, Horseshoe Station was passed, later Gilman's Ranch, always onward, to Fort Kearny, Liberty Farm, Granada, unceasingly eastward the Pony pressed forward. By the late afternoon of the 13th, in the promised 10 days from San Francisco, the expressman on the last relay (again, Richardson or Fry?) boarded the ferry at Elwood, Kansas, and crossed the Missouri to St. Joseph.

Waiting for him at the riverbank, athrill with anticipation, was a noisy assembly of townspeople. He was greeted with loud cheers and the clanging of church bells. At the Patee House, where the company had its office, the cannon again boomed a thunderous salute, while local militiamen, dressed in uniform, paraded the streets and fired their rifles. Bonfires and fireworks added to the combustive celebration.

Meanwhile, the westbound express, which had passed the St. Joseph-bound Pony east of Salt Lake City, raced on through the Utah Territory, checking in at Egan's Canyon, Ruby Valley, Roberts Creek, Cold Springs, Sand Springs, Buckland's Station, and reached Carson City Thursday, April 12, at 3:30 p.m. While news of the arrival was being flashed ahead over F. A. Bee's telegraph line, Warren Upson flung the *mochila* over his waiting horse, dug in his spurs, and was off for a return ride to Genoa, 15 miles away, then Woodford's, another 18, and on over the summit, passing a flood-wave of humanity, vehicles and animals which, now that the blizzard was over, had burst upon the trail in a frenzied rush to Washoe.

His ride was finished at Sportsman Hall, well down the western slope of the mountains, where he had started his eastward trip 11 days previously. From there the ride of his relief, William Hamilton, has already been traced to Sacramento and to the tumultuous reception tendered him on arrival.

When the big paddle wheels of the *Antelope* began to churn the river as she warped away from her mooring and headed downstream to San Francisco, it was precisely 5:45 p.m. Safely and comfortably aboard, Hamilton would have nearly seven hours of blissful rest while the ship steamed down river to the city by the Golden Gate.

There he was to be surprised by another reception, which, for excitement and boisterousness, would quite equal the uproarious welcome that had engulfed him in Sacramento. Since the previous evening, when a telegraph dispatch told of the Pony's arrival at Carson City, San Franciscans began organizing for the big event.

Newspaper reporters had offered the use of their Reporters' Union Hall, behind the City Hall, for a meeting place. Invited were Major P. L. Solomon, the U. S. Marshal; Charles Crane, the agent, and A. S. Gould, the secretary, of the Overland Telegraph Co. In turn, these gentlemen invited numerous guests from the local offices of the government agencies, the State and Alta telegraph lines, as well as the Butterfield Overland Mail Company, "and other gentlemen who have been particularly forward in advocating overland communication."

At 7:30 p.m. the Hall was filled, and Messrs. Crane and Solomon welcomed the guests with "a number" of baskets of champagne. Wit and humor were soon flowing freely, and the Pony Express was toasted with great enthusiasm.

Solomon, Crane and William V. Wells were named a nominating committee to select a citizens committee at large to organize the reception for the following day. After a short

A rare view of the Hannibal & St. Joseph Railroad's woodburner, "Missouri", which brought the first Pony mail from the east into St. Joseph — over two hours late.

The river steamer *Denver* in which the first Pony rider was carried across the Missouri River from St. Joseph to Elwood, Kansas.

The steamer *New World* in which the first eastbound Pony Express mail from San Francisco was carried to Sacramento.

Mrs. William Baumhoff

Sportsman Hall in the 1860's, starting place of Warren Upson's epic ride with the first eastbound express.

Mormon Tavern, near Clarksville, California, on the old White Rock Road followed by the Pony on early trips between Sacramento and Placerville.

Jane Voiles Collection

Remains of substantial old stone structure at Schell Creek, Nevada, a Pony
Express stop near the Utah border, later renamed Fort Schellbourne.

The original barn at Strawberry, the fourth horse-relay stop in the mountains east of Placerville,
California.

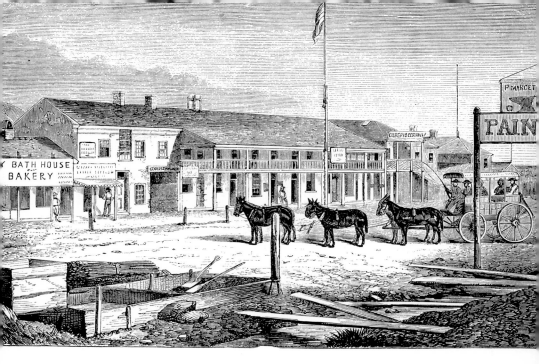

Salt Lake House, on Main Street, Salt Lake City, where Pony riders were domiciled. The hostelry attracted "a rough-looking crowd of drivers, drivers' friends, and idlers, almost every man armed with revolver and bowie-knife."

"California Pony Express," an early drawing showing the *mochila*.

Aaron Stein del

Pony Express stable at St. Joseph, Missouri.

Cottonwood Station, Kansas, built in 1857 by G. H. Hollenberg. Now a local memorial, the place in its heyday served as an important stop for stagecoaches and express riders.

caucus the trio declared they had picked 19 men, plus the president and members of the board of supervisors. Included in their committee panel were C. L. Weller, postmaster; Frederick Mac-Crellish, publisher of the *Alta;* James Gamble of the State Telegraph Co.; William Buckley, superintendent of the Butterfield line (Russell, Majors & Waddell's chief competitor!); and Joseph Lambert, agent of the Alta Telegraph Co., who later was to be designated San Francisco agent for the Pony Express.

The roster was quickly approved and this action occasioned another round of toasts. One was given to "Major F. A. Bee" of overland fame. Someone toasted "The memory of Henry Clay," it being his birthday. Glasses were raised to "The citizens of St. Louis [sic], who are now celebrating the arrival there of the Pony Express from this city." Another was to "Major P. L. Solomon." He eloquently responded: "The mustang ponies of California; they have done more for civilization with California boys on their backs than their mailed ancestors did in conquering the Montezumas."

At the Chamber of Commerce the next day the citizens committee met twice. MacCrellish was elected chairman and William V. Wells secretary. Although they knew the Pony's arrival would be at a late hour, committee members agreed to hold the celebration whenever it was. Word was sent out to the various theaters about the city, where announcements were made from the stage.

About 11 p.m. the California Band began a musical migration through the streets, and attracted a large assemblage, "all on the *qui vive*," to welcome the incoming rider. The crowd made the round of the various fire houses, picking up delegates from each, "until the procession swelled with constant additions from all points to not far from 2,000. But for the lateness of the hour this number would have been more than trebled."

Bonfires were now blazing merrily in many of the streets, and the personnel of the otherwise fire-conscious engine houses let the flames become so lurid against the midnight sky that an "alarm of fire" was pealed out from the City Hall bell.

The huge procession headed down to the Broadway wharf, where, during a half-hour wait for the *Antelope,* the California Band kept spirits high and enthusiasm at a peak by offering selections of martial airs and waltzes. At 12:38 a.m. the *Antelope* tied up at the dock and the procession formed into the following order of march:

California Band playing "See the Conquering Hero Comes"

Engine Company No. 2
Hook and Ladder Company No. 2
Engine Company No. 5
Engine Company No. 6

The above companies had their machines
full manned and many of them lighted,
and the men bearing torches.

THE PONY EXPRESS
(A bay horse with Spanish saddle, the
mochila stuffed with letters brought
overland.)

Citizens on foot and mounted

On arrival at the Alta Telegraph office, Montgomery and Merchant Streets, Charles Crane, grand marshal of the parade, called a halt and a series of rousing cheers were raised for the Pony Express. It seems that several speeches were planned, but it was decided that in this yawning hour—it was past 1:00 a.m.—welcoming addresses could be dispensed with. However, the spirit of the affair carried on "until the 'wee sma' hours,' the boys 'running' in various boisterous styles and harmless ways," according to the wonderfully detailed account of the celebration carried in the *Alta*.

Chapter Six

MAKING THE HEADLINES

THE FOURTH ESTATE of California's early years was a no-holds-barred vocation in which the moral qualities, accuracy and objectiveness of one newspaper were held to be fair game for public ridicule in the columns of a competing sheet. Charges of plagiarism were rife, yet nearly every paper throughout the state copied, as a matter of course, items from other news journals. Cribbing was particularly evident on current out-of-state news, originating largely in letters from paid correspondents. These were employed by the papers which could afford them, in principal cities of the eastern states.

Until the 20-day Butterfield Overland Mail was inaugurated, contributions from correspondents were forwarded via the Isthmus of Panama, making the arrival of every steamer at San Francisco a news event of major proportions. It wasn't so much the speed of the Butterfield line (approximately equal to that of the Panama route) as it was the stage company's more frequent, twice-a-week schedule that caused it to find especial favor in the eyes of California publishers. Its overland route was a means of halving the time between news making and news printing.

And so, with the astounding promise of the Pony Express to again cut the time in half, it was a natural consequence that the daring courier service found editorial shelter and encouragement in all segments of the California press, indeed, of the nation's press. Heartened by the ultimate hope it held for telegraph and railroad, newspapermen found a temptation with this new bird in hand to draw an odious comparison with the established and proven service over the southern land route.

Something smacking of that was in a test of speed between the Butterfield line and the Pony Express, made by the enterprising St. Louis correspondent of the Sacramento *Union*. On the day of the Pony's first departure for the West he caused identical letters to be forwarded by express *mochila* and the Butterfield stage. When the Pony mail arrived in Sacramento April 14th, the *Union*, with restrained glee, reported that nothing had been heard of the letter by stage. "The conclusion is," the paper observed triumphantly, "that with all the admirable appointments of Butterfield & Co., on the southern route, it has been fairly and handsomely distanced."

Of all the state's newspapers the *Union* was especially solicitous of the Pony's welfare, giving its readers reports of the express' passing at various points along the route, praising its accomplishments in delivering a story, always being careful to credit the Pony for news that it brought, and anxiously exhorting subscribers to lend it more liberal support.

"The Pony Express for the East left San Francisco yesterday afternoon at 4 o'clock," the paper dutifully reported of the fourth trip. "It took 75 letters from San Francisco and up to the hour of 9 o'clock last evening, there were 18 from Sacramento. This is something of a falling off from last week. Californians must do better than this . . ."

But no paper had a corner on praise for the Pony, and not a few were positively gushing. Take this sample from the St. Joseph *Free Democrat:*

"They [the Pony's footprints] are in California, leaping over its golden sands, treading its busy streets. The courser has unrolled to us the great American panorama, allowed us to glance at the home of one million people, and has put a girdle around the earth in 40 minutes. Verily the riding is like the riding of Jehu, the son of Nimshi, for he rideth furiously. Take out your watch. We are eight days from New York, 18 from London. The race is to the swift."

In more restrained prose, the *Rocky Mountain News* of Denver editorialized in this strain on the company's management:

". . . it stands today, probably, the best fitted, best stocked and best managed route of the same magnitude in the world . . . Unlike the Butterfield route, with its subsidy of $600,000 per year for carrying the mails, this colossal enterprise has been built up and is wholly sustained by individual enterprise . . . Its projector and president, William H. Russell, well deserved the name of 'Napoleon of the West'."

The press out West, more urgently than its counterpart in the East, sought greater patronage of the Pony so as to sustain the new lifeline of news, thus helping to end the isolated existence of people on the Pacific shore. The San Francisco *Evening Bulletin,* plumping for support, addressed its commercial readers from a very unique angle:

"As a means of friendly correspondence, it is too expensive, but our business men, we believe, will soon find the five dollars paid on each letter carried by the Pony a profitable investment. In making remittances, 10 days time at least will be saved; and in a country like ours, where money readily commands two per cent per month, this will not be lost sight of."

As early as February 28, 1860, scarcely a month after Russell's decision to start a horse express, it was rumored that he had stolen the idea from John Butterfield. The rumor persisted, and in the latter part of May, Mr. Allen (not of Samuel & Allen), Butterfield's agent at St. Louis, revealed a startling proposal of the Overland Mail people. They were, he informed the local correspondent of the *Bulletin,* going to launch their own pony express. The telegraph was soon to reach Fort Smith, Arkansas, he explained. The new pony service would span the distance between that point and Los Angeles, the proposed western terminal of the wire. It was a 1,500-mile stretch which Butterfield, he asserted, planned to cover in only five days Pony time, or at the fantastic rate of 300 miles a day.

The *Bulletin's* militant and partisan-minded correspondent thought that over and then, in an uninhibited burst of imagery, delivered himself of the most ebullient piece of journalism about the Pony Express that was ever inked on newsprint.

Unequivocally he stated that Russell, Majors & Waddell would "fill the gap" (he failed to say which gap) in only four and a half days' time, and that if the telegraph company did not extend its line westward, "the Central Express will build a line of its own."

The company, he said, "has a capital of $1,000,000 [more correctly, it was at the door of bankruptcy] and is running its line for glory. If the line pays its expenses it is well; if it pays a profit, it is better; but if it does not ever pay expenses, it is all the same—the company can stand the brunt, and what is more will stand it. It is their purpose to establish on a firm basis the pre-eminence of the Central Route over all others, and there is no such word as fail with those gentlemen." Amen and Halleluiah!

All this plethoric journalism gave the Pony Express not only a good send-off but sustained its momentum, and lent it moral aid to carry through the trying days ahead. For the nonce, the courier service reciprocated, holding to regular departures and keeping within tolerable limits of the promised 10-day transit across country.

Following the first departure from St. Joseph, on Tuesday, it was announced that subsequent trips would leave on Fridays, at 9 o'clock in the morning. At San Francisco the switch to Fridays was made on the third departure.

The second trip, on April 13th from St. Joseph, was significant. During this ride there occurred, like an ominous warning of dire circumstances awaiting the Pony if it persisted, the first instance of Indian trouble. At the time, newspapers gave it little notice, succinctly reporting that the express was delayed six hours at Roberts Creek by marauding Indians who had driven off the horses at the station. Despite the holdup, the chain of riders completed the trip in but 10 days and one hour, and delivered the mail at San Francisco at 10 a.m., April 23rd.

Helping speed the riders was an innovation in the route effected by William W. Finney the previous night, perhaps on telegraphic advice from Carson City that the Pony would be late. Between Sacramento and Oakland he stocked the road with horses and made preparations to forward the mail by land, instead of river steamer. An unidentified rider brought the express into Sacramento at 1 a.m., April 23rd, and the mail "proceeded at once by relays of horses, with Hamilton as rider, to San Francisco, via Benicia, Martinez and Oakland," the *Union* recorded.

Hamilton approximately followed the winding Sacramento River westward to Benicia where he arrived at 7 a.m. At that point Thomas J. Bedford, a local lad, took the *mochila* and boarded Captain O. C. Coffin's steam ferry boat, the *Carquinez*. The good skipper, by previous arrangement, agreeably had berthed his vessel at this early hour so that the Pony would lose no time waiting for the 10-minute ride across the river.

In Martinez, on the opposite shore, the *Contra Costa Gazette* reported:

". . . not a moment of time was lost in conveying it to this place. As the boat touched this side the horse sprang from her deck, and dashing up the wharf was soon lost to sight, as he and his gallant rider went flying on their way to Oakland. The distance from Martinez to Oakland is about 25 miles. The Express left here at 7:33 a.m., and arrived at Oakland, as reported to us, at 9:32, which, if correct, makes the time occupied one hour and 59 minutes. According to the city papers, however, it was accomplished in one hour and 45 minutes, which probably was the swiftest riding on the whole route."

Precisely the road that Tom Bedford took to Oakland was not related, but it is likely that he followed the principal route then being regularly traveled by J. Bamber & Co.'s Express, whose stagecoaches were on daily runs from Martinez to Oakland, via Pacheco, Walnut Creek House, Alamo and Lafayette.

From Oakland "a great crowd of people" rode over on the boat with the expressman to San Francisco. There, giving due notice to Bedford's extraordinary speed, the *Bulletin*, with tongue in cheek, remarked that "the Pony did not shed his shoes, his rider did not break his neck, nor was there any appreciable smell of fire upon his garments when he came in."

But the effort was disappointing in the end result. Complainingly, the paper added, "Very few letters brought the Pony. Dreadful slow people live on the other side of the mountains."

The substitution of horses for river steamer was of short duration. One more trip, the third from St. Joseph, leaving Friday, April 20th, followed the land route to Oakland. By the time the fourth westbound express reached Sacramento, the horses beyond the city had been withdrawn, Finney having determined that, after all, conveyance by boat would meet the need just as well. And it did, until March of the next year, when a rider missed the Sacramento steamer and the *mochila* was dispatched overland to San Francisco. Three months later the Pony, then under new management, reverted to the river road and expressmen galloped over it regularly.

In June, 1860, the General Agent of the Pacific made another, more permanent change in mode of travel, this time east of Sacramento. Until then, the Pony Express, coming into the city, had followed the White Rock road from Placerville. What happened now may come as a shock to horse lovers and dedicated followers of Pony lore. Finney decided that the mail would ride the iron horse of the Sacramento Valley Railroad between Sacramento and Folsom, a distance of 22 miles.

The change was ideal from the standpoints of efficiency and economy. In Sacramento the rail line's depot was close by the Alta Telegraph office, which served as the local Pony Express agency; and at Folsom the train station was almost directly opposite the Wells, Fargo agency, operated by Palmer & Day, gold assayers, a suitable office for the Pony. East of Folsom the route was laid along the Mormon Island-Green Valley section of the Overland Road to Placerville. The intervening distance required but one remount station, which was arranged for at the Pleasant Grove House, a roadside inn on a quarter-section farm, just 10 miles from Folsom. Here the proprietor, Ira Rounds Sanders, also contracted to shoe the horses of the express.

The unique arrangement didn't eliminate any riders, but did release the horses at three remount stations along the White Rock road. These were then sorely needed in the Utah Territory where raiding Pah-Utes were busy running off stock from Pony stations all across the desert.

Precisely when the mail took to the trains is not known. The first clear, rather matter-of-fact mention of the substitution is given in the Sacramento *Union* of June 30th where the Pony's expected arrival at Folsom is reported to be "in time for the noon cars." Many similar notations were made concerning later trips. However, earlier, on June 3rd, the paper reported arrival of the express from Carson City, "continuing its course by land" to Sacramento—a terminology not previously used except to describe the temporary running of horses into Oakland. Whether this was pure verbiage, or a means of denoting a change from intended plans to employ the rail facility is left unanswered.

At any rate, Finney had already left for the Indian-troubled area, stopping long enough at Placerville on June 1st to wire back instructions postponing departure of the express the same day. From another telegram he filed at Carson City, it is evident that he took with him some stock. At this juncture he was without funds to buy horses for replenishing the stations raided by the Pah-Utes, so it is concluded they came from a rearrangement of relay points. On his trip over the Sierras, a similar shuffle in stations seems to have been made between Lake Bigler (Tahoe) and Genoa, for about this time Friday's station, operated by Martin "Friday" Burke and James W. Small, appears in the record in lieu of Woodford's.

One of the problems bound to arise in patronizing the rail line lay in matching the approximate schedule of horseflesh with the rigid timetable of the steamcars. In the office of Henry B. Waddilove, Folsom agent of the Sacramento Valley Railroad, departing trains for Sacramento were listed at 6:30 a.m., 12 noon and 5:15 p.m. Any holdup or delay on the part of the Pony in getting into Folsom, causing the express to miss one of these trains—and probably the river steamers at Sacramento with which the railroad connected—would forestall the mail's progress all the way to San Francisco.

In December, 1860, the *Union* complained of this very difficulty. The telegraph line to Fort Churchill was suffering one of its recurrent failures. The weather and stagecoach drivers are said to have abetted one another in causing the breakdowns. The latter, finding a section of wire blown to the ground, were known to have clipped pieces to repair a broken spoke or wheel hub, blandly explaining they thought the wire was provided for such an emergency.

This time, as usual, the westbound rider left his dispatches to be sent ahead from the Fort. By the time the Pony reached Folsom, late for the train, the dispatches had not yet been sent. The disappointed *Union* heaped abuse on the poor telegraph service, and bitterly observed that the express would have beat the telegraph all the way to Sacramento, had either the cars been running or the horses placed along the route.

Chapter Seven

INDIANS ON THE WARPATH

ANGRY, rampaging Indians forced an abrupt halt to the pounding hooves, even before the shuttling Pony had time to live up to the glowing promises of the nation's impulsive press. From the outset, the threat of Indian attack had been real and always present and, indeed, was provided for in the heavy armament allotted the mounted couriers. Yet, until now, it had remained just that—a threat. No rider had suffered at the hands of the savages, no mail had been lost. The chief concern had been to guard the stations and equipment and stock against the thieving proclivities of the redskin.

Presently, in the western reaches of Utah Territory (let's call the area what it was soon to become—Nevada Territory), the valiant Pony was to have the doubtful distinction of being tinder for a holocaust of murderous warfare between white man and red savage. The deadly conflict was to borrow a page from the gruesome history of other Indian wars, with blood spilling over sand and sagebrush from the head-on collision of a restless civilization with an ancient and static culture. At the crossroads were misunderstanding, mistrust and hate.

One of the earliest contacts between whites and Indians of Nevada occurred in August, 1832. The greeting was a rifle ball. Milton Sublette, with a company of trappers, had reached the headwaters of the Humboldt. There a cousin-by-marriage of President-to-be James K. Polk displayed a peculiar brand of heroism. Joe Meek, a free-trapper member of the party, coolly fired at and killed a Shoshone. N. J. Wyeth, a Yankee mountaineer accompanying the group, questioned Meek about the incident, according to an account in Mrs. F. F. Victor's story, *The River of the West.*

Meek told him that he had killed the native "as a hint to keep the Indians from stealing our traps."

"Had he stolen any?" Wyeth asked.

"No," replied Meek, "but he looked as if he was going to."

In the following year Joseph Walker headed an exploring and trapping expedition, organized by Captain B. L. E. Bonneville (again Meek was with the company). The party was slowly making its way along the Humboldt, trapping as it went, when it was discovered that a group of curious Indians were following. The savages maintained a prudent distance and kept clear of the line of the trappers' advance. Day by day their number grew, and by night a few of the more daring young braves sneaked into Walker's camp, carrying off trifling articles, that, to their infantile minds, were precious treasure.

"At length, one day," recounted Washington Irving, "they —the trappers—came to the banks of a stream emptying into Ogden's River which they were obliged to ford. Here a great number of Shoshones were posted on the opposite bank. Persuaded that they were there with hostile intent, they advanced upon them, leveling their rifles, and killed 25 of them on the spot. The rest fled a short distance, then halted and turned about, howling and whining like wolves and uttering the most piteous wailings. The trappers chased them in every direction; the poor wretches made no defense, but fled with terror; neither does it appear from the account of the boasted victors, that a weapon had been wielded or a weapon launched by the Indians throughout the affair. We feel perfectly convinced that the poor savages had no hostile intention, but had merely gathered together through motives of curiosity."

Perhaps so. But to white men on unknown ground strange savages with strange ways were apt to be enemies before they became friends, and scalping was a horrible way to die.

For 17 years following the departure of Walker's expedition, Nevada was relatively free of conflict. Then came the human tidal wave of 1849-50 that swept across the Great Basin, over the Sierras and spread upon the goldfields of California. Among these immigrants and those who followed were reckless, ignorant individuals in whose warped opinion heroism was attained by the wanton killing of Indians. Repeated incidents of inhumanity and oppression brought retaliation from the natives for both real and fancied aggressions, and the various tribes of the Shoshones rode the warpath until 1863, raiding immigrant trains, burning settlements and attacking the mail services.

The winter of 1859-60—the season which made a hero out of Pony Rider Warren Upson—brought storms of unprecedented severity. Only the summer before, the Indians, who were accustomed to the passage of westbound gold-seekers, began to witness a turnabout, as the first surge of California diggers retraced their way to the new and fabulously rich promise of the Comstock. Thoroughly upset by actual and imagined wrongs inflicted by the hordes of intruding whites, the red man was easily persuaded that the great evil spirit was angered, and had sent the storms which were freezing and starving his kinfolk.

So it happened that Nevadans, if not surprised, were shocked and alarmed when Dexter E. Deming was murdered. On January 13, 1860, a group of Indians crept to his unlocked cabin near Honey Lake Valley, and waited inside for the settler to return from a practice run on a pair of new snowshoes. As Deming approached the cabin door, he was hit by a double blast from his own two shotguns. The savages dragged his body inside, stripped it and dropped it into a small cellar. They then ransacked the cabin, stole two horses and raced away.

Dexter's brother, Jack, returning from Toadtown, discovered the atrocity and made an immediate about face to carry the grisly news back to the tiny settlement. Ninety-two enraged citizens of the area promptly filed a petition with the provisional governor of Nevada, Isaac Roop, demanding that he call out the military forces and "chastise the Indians."

Creditably to himself, Roop instead calmly ordered Lieutenant U. T. Tutt, one of the petitioners, to head a detachment to track down the murderers and ascertain their tribe. Tutt and his party did so, tracking the killers on foot through deep snow, and returned to report that he had followed them to a Pah-Ute camp.

Thereupon Roop named two commissioners, Captain William Weatherlow, who headed the Honey Lake Valley Rangers, and T. J. Harvey, whose home would be burned by the Indians before July. They were to counsel with Chief Winnemucca of the Pah-Utes and bring back the guilty redskins. Surrender of the murderers was in accordance with a treaty previously made with the Indian chief.

But the tribesmen were in an ugly mood. At first, they refused to tell the whereabouts of Winnemucca, and then deliberately misguided the two men. At one point the emissaries were captured and temporarily held prisoners. Eventually they located the chief, but found him adamant. Not only did he refuse to turn over the killers, or to use his prestige to prevent further depredations, he demanded that the whites pay him $16,000 for usurping Honey Lake Valley.

By the end of April the Indians were destitute and their tempers were aflame. The Pah-Ute tribe had gathered for a

powwow at Pyramid Lake, a reservation, to vent their griev-
ances and to decide upon a course of action. The air, filled with
vengeance and hate for the whites, was fanned hot by the
imprecations of young braves.

Of that branch of the tribe living on the reservation an
Indian named Numaga was the chosen chief. White men called
him "Young Winnemucca," the war chief, but he was not. There
was only one general chief—Old Winnemucca, whose Indian
name was Po-i-to. Numaga was an Indian statesman, intellec-
tual, eloquent and courageous, an impressive figure standing
six feet tall, with a Roman nose and broad chin and firm mouth,
marking a character of strong will and decision. He had lived
among the whites in California, could speak English, and was
well aware of the numerical and material superiority of the race
against whom his people would unleash the arrow. In the closing days of April he rode from camp to camp, from family to
family, and from friend to friend, urging and beseeching them
to decide against war.

At last, in May, all the chiefs of the tribe sat in council.
Numaga remained silent, waiting to the last, listening and
weighing the arguments. When all had spoken he arose and
began an impassioned plea to avert bloodshed and to find the
way to peace.

At this moment of eloquence there dashed up to the council
an Indian on a foam-flecked pony. Moguannoga, the rider
declared, with nine braves, had burned Williams' Station on
the Carson River the previous night, and killed four whites.

All the steam and passion faded from Numaga. Sadly he
turned to the chiefs and counseled against further talk. It was
now time to prepare for war; surely, the soldiers would come
to fight.

James O. Williams kept the station, which Samuel S. Buckland called Honey Lake Smith's Station, at the big bend of
the Carson River, the first Pony relay east of Buckland's own

ranch. What act at this tiny speck of civilization caused it to become the tinderbox of a full-scale Indian war was an arguable question among Williams' contemporaries. He himself had no testimony to offer, having been camping that night, May 7th, about two miles down river.

In California the newspapers quoted Osmer Darst, a resident of Gold Hill, near Virginia City, as saying that "an old Indian went to Williams' house with a squaw, when four white men tied the Indian and then committed an atrocious outrage upon the woman. They then let the Indian go. He afterwards came back with other Indians, and put a white woman who was in the house, out of doors, and also three white men who had nothing to do with the outrage. They then bound the four white men who abused the squaw, and burned them in the house."

Darst said his facts came from the white woman, "now stopping at Silver City." The next day's issue of the Sacramento *Union*, however, published a private letter vigorously denying any charges of immorality. But years later Editor William Wright of the *Territorial Enterprise* at Virginia City, reiterated the involvement of the men with the squaws—two of them— adding that the husband of one went to Moguannoga (or, as the whites called him, Captain Soo) for help.

Twenty years after the raid three of Moguannoga's raiding party were still living. To get a firsthand account of the killing, Thompson & West, publishers of *History of Nevada*, employed a professional writer, who, in company with Major W. H. H. Wasson, Acting Indian Agent, traveled to Pyramid Lake and obtained an interpreter named George Quip. Through him they interviewed one of the survivors, and the following account was written:

> "We get there 'bout night; sun little way up; and leave ponies back, maybe half mile. Then we all go down to cabin, and three white men come out. They look mighty scared, and talk heap to Captain Soo, and—"

Palmer & Day's assay office at Folsom was the Pony agency
after June, 1860. The mail was transferred from here to the
Sacramento Valley Railroad across the street.

Steamcars crossing the railroad bridge over the American River at Folsom. This was the route taken
by the Pony mail into Sacramento when Folsom became the terminus of the express riders' trail.

Society of California Pioneers

The original, still occupied Pleasant Grove House, the only Pony remount station between Folsom and Placerville.

Pony Express blacksmith's firebox at Pleasant Grove House.

Ruins of the Cold Springs station in Nevada, made famous by the legendary ride of "Pony Bob" Haslam. He tells of relaying horses at this desolate spot while making a ride with eastbound mail at the very height of the murderous Indian attacks. Retracing his run the next day, he found the redskins had visited in the interim, massacred the keeper and drove off the station's stock.

Charles Kelly

Fish Springs station in Utah as it appeared in 1930, still with a sod roof. In September, 1860, the station keeper was a German Swiss, who had, "to little purpose", previously dug for gold in California.

Rush Valley station, kept by J. H. Faust, who was described by a traveler as "a civil and communicative man, who added a knowledge of books and drugs to local history." He later became a physician. Station was 20 miles west of Camp Floyd.

Charles Kelly

"What did they say to him?" we asked.

"Dunno; talk heap. I no understand English then."

"Well, what did they do next?"

"Bimeby one start off and run up the road towards Buck-land's, and two Injun run after him, and bring him back. Then one, he run for the river, and me after him; he jump in, and me watch; bimeby he get half-way across maybe, then drown."

"Did you shoot him when he was swimming?"

"No; nobody shoot him in water; maybe so, somebody shoot him 'fore that. He heap splatter water; no swim much. I know him drown purty soon; no use to shoot."

"While you were gone to the river what was done at the station?"

"I no see that. They tell me white man draw a knife, and then one Injun grab him from behind, then two, three—maybe four—Indian grab him; then one take his arm and do so, and break it, and that make him drop the knife; and then they throw him on the ground, and kill him."

"How did they kill him?"

"They no tell me that. I dunno; maybe choke him."

"How did they kill the other man?"

"Dunno. When I come back, four Injun hold him on the ground; then I go off down the river little ways, to find a place to picket pony, and when I look back, see cabin on fire."

"Was it dark when they burned the station?"

"No—purty near dark, though."

The narrator insisted that they found but three whites at the station. We said to him that five men were killed, and he asked:

"How you know?"

Upon his being told that the information was from those who buried them, he replied that, "Maybe white man tell you heap of lies." Finally, he suggested that it was possible that two might have remained in the house concealed; who were suffocated and perished in the flames. The following are the names of the parties who were killed, and no one escaped from the place:

Oscar Williams, a married man, aged 33 years, and a native of Maine.

David Williams, a single man, aged 22 years, and a native of Maine.

Samuel Sullivan, a married man, aged 25 years, and a native of New York.

John Flemming, a single man, aged 25 years, and a native of New York.

"Dutch Phil"; unknown name, age, and residence.

The Indians [continued the Thompson & West account] camped on the bottom around the place until 2 or 3 o'clock in the morning, and then started across the eight-mile desert for Buckland's station, intending to kill the owner, after whom it is named. They passed by the ranch of C. M. Davis without molesting him, and on arriving at daylight on the farm of W. H. Bloomfield, one of their number named———, proposed to the band that they drive off the stock from the place and return to the lake without committing any further depredations. It now being daylight, and as a further advance would be attended by considerable risk, it was determined to follow this suggestion; and one of their number was sent in advance to report what they had been doing. It was the arrival upon the council ground at Pyramid Lake, of this messenger, that interrupted Numaga's speech.

"Why," we asked, "did you not kill C. M. Davis; he was much nearer to you than S. S. Buckland?"

"Davis," he replied, "purty good man; never whip Injun; mighty cross all the time; we all say no kill him, purty good."

On the evening of the massacre, the owner of the station, J. O. Williams, was camping a couple of miles further up the river, and thus escaped the fate of his brothers.

The next morning he returned, and finding his place a smouldering ruin, around which lay the bodies of his murdered kinsmen, he started for Virginia City.

Williams' announcement electrified the mining community, and word raced like the wind to other settlements in the Washoe region. The reaction was immediate. Pah-Utes, illiterate, unkempt, reduced to little more than scavengers of pine nuts, were scorned and despised by the whites. In this atmosphere hate was easily catapulted into revenge, as armed companies were organized at Genoa, Carson City, Silver City and

Virginia City. Major William M. Ormsby, who had been an agent for the Pioneer Stage Line, led the contingent at Genoa. W. C. Marley, then keeper of Buckland's Pony Express Station, joined the Carson City group.

Converging on Buckland's, the volunteers—105 strong—gave every indication that they held little regard for the fighting capabilities of the Indians, the procession taking on the light-hearted aspect of a sportsmen's outing. After proceeding to Williams' Station, where graves were dug for the five dead men, the impromptu brigade set out for Pyramid Lake. Along the way the men amused themselves chanting the slogan, "An Indian for breakfast and a pony to ride," being a jovial allusion to victory and the spoils of war. No one seemed to worry that this "heterogeneous mixture of independent elements, poorly armed, without discipline," had no leader. Major Ormsby had urged that an over-all commander be chosen, but the suggestion was carelessly disregarded.

Blithely, the party approached the southern end of Pyramid Lake. Ahead lay a strip of sage-covered bottom land and a clump of cottonwood trees. Beyond, in the distance, the volunteers spied a number of Indian warriors stationed on a rise of ground, and set off in pursuit. But brashly the Pah-Utes firmly stood their ground, and as the whites drew near, showered them with arrows. This hot reception was unexpected and caught the gay bravados off guard. Cautiously, they began a withdrawal toward the cottonwoods, to consolidate and reorganize.

Then the trap snapped shut. From behind every sage bush and out of the cottonwood grove sprung a horde of frenzied, screaming warriors. Utter panic ensued. Trapped and terrified by the deadly ambush, the citizen-soldiers fled in complete rout, the charging, battle-crazed savages hot after them. Over 20 of their number fell as they madly raced southward, over the way they had come, trying to reach the safety of higher ground. Mercilessly, the Pah-Utes pressed the fight. Attack, attack,

attack. Twenty more whites fell to the savage wrath before the nightmare ended.

It was one of the gravest catastrophes in the history of Indian warfare. Major Ormsby, helped to his saddle after being seriously wounded, refused to go on and become a burden to his fleeing comrades. Instead, he tried to surrender, but was summarily killed and his body rolled into a ravine. When survivors of the battle straggled into Buckland's Station, the news of the disaster spread quickly. Throughout Carson Valley the settlers sought safety in the most substantially-built homes and threw up fortifications.

Meanwhile, new commands of volunteers again were hastily formed. General Clarke of the Department of California ordered 150 men to march for Nevada. Several hundred civilians came out of California mining towns to augment a large contingent organized at Carson City under Colonel John C. Hayes. Samuel Buckland formed a company of volunteers who placed themselves under Captain Rowe.

On May 26th a force of about 800 men—Army soldiers and private citizens—took the trail from Carson City for Pyramid Lake. Not far from Williams' Station they encountered the Indians and in a brief battle a half-dozen Pah-Utes and two white men were killed. Winnemucca ordered his warriors to retreat and, with the whites in pursuit, withdrew to the proximity of the disastrous battle a fortnight earlier. The bodies of the unburied volunteers could still be seen lying where they had fallen.

The cagey old chief defiantly perched his forces on the vantage point of a ledge near the previous battlefield and waited for the whites. Col. Hayes launched a determined attack which lasted over three hours, finally flushing Winnemucca off the ledge and forcing his savages to flee into the hills. A spirited chase followed in which, by nightfall, the whites had dropped 25 Pah-Utes with gunfire. The next day the chase was resumed, finally being abandoned after sundown. Col. Hayes directed the volunteers, who were on a 10-day enlistment, to return to Carson City for mustering out.

And so the issue had been joined and settled. Numaga's fears were proven correct: Pah-Ute bravery could not hold the field against the superiority of the white man. Still, while the battle was over, the war was not. Pah-Utes, Gosh-Utes and other branches of the Shoshone tribe, remaining hostile and unsubdued, were to hack away at the white man for long months to come, pillaging, burning and murdering in hit-and-run tactics all across the breadth of Nevada Territory.

Unprotected and vulnerable, the string of Pony Express stations lay invitingly across the path of this intermittent rampage, like tender morsels to be snatched in the claws of a diving hawk. Even while Col. Hayes was organizing his army at Carson City, the Indians gave effective notice of their intentions. At San Francisco William W. Finney received a dispatch from the Washoe capital advising that the station at Simpson's Park, 135 miles east of Carson City, between Cold Springs and Dry Creek, had been attacked and razed on May 20th.

Promptly, Finney sought out General Clarke and implored the aid of 75 soldiers to be posted at stations between Sand Springs and Dry Creek. The general declined, regretting that, despite the vital importance of the mail route, the limited number of men under his command—already depleted by the 150 soldiers sent to Col. Hayes—eliminated any possibility of help.

Apparently Finney had not fully awakened to the critical situation, nor guessed the threatened ravages against the Pony mail, until he had read the telegram. The fifth eastbound mail trip which departed San Francisco May 3rd, had already cleared Williams' Station before Moguannoga's raid, May 7th. Subsequent trips were dispatched Friday, May 10th, and Friday, May 17th.

The latter trip might better have been cancelled. When the rider rode into Salt Lake City, he carried no mail and reported that two riders had been killed. On a waybill handed to the relieving rider, the Salt Lake City agent noted, "May 24—Rider just in. The Indians have chased all the men from the stations between Diamond Springs and Carson Valley. The *mochila* is lost."

Fully alarmed now by the Simpson's Park incident, Finney set out for the troubled area. Further word, underlining the gravity of the situation, must have reached him en route, for at Placerville, he wired his instructions for postponement of the June 1st trip.

Three days later, in Carson City, the general agent apprised himself of the disrupted state of affairs and realized it would be hopeless to reinstitute service without strong support. To Messrs. Burton and McCarty, Sacramento merchants, who probably were substantial customers of the express, or suppliers of Pony equipment and provisions, he sent the following wire:

"Will Sacramento help the Pony in its difficulty? We have conferred some benefits, have asked but little, and perhaps the people will assist. Can anything be done in your city towards paying expenses to furnish arms and provisions for 25 men to go through with me to Salt Lake to take and bring on the Express? I will be responsible for the return of the arms—will have transportation of my own, and can get men here. What is wanted is $1,000 for the pay of the men, $500 for provisions, and 20 Sharpe's rifles, and as many dragoon pistols. I will guarantee to keep the Pony alive a while longer. Wm. W. Finney."

Sacramentans were quick to respond, generously raising $1,200 to $1,500. San Francisco got in on the act, too, when a wire was sent to Frederick MacCrellish of the *Alta*. He replied that of course, the people of that city would contribute, and that the *Alta* and another donor had already pledged $100 apiece.

The prompt assistance enabled Finney to organize and outfit a party of 20 men to repair the broken links in the chain of stations and restock them with provisions and animals. Inconveniently, at the last minute, he became indisposed and had to relinquish leadership to Bolivar Roberts. The May 25th mail from San Francisco had been halted at Carson City, and taking these letters along, Roberts set out at two p.m., June 9th, his party "well armed and mounted." Invited to go along was Postmaster Morrell of Salt Lake City.

Seven days later, after having dropped off seven men at stations along the way, the contingent reached Roberts Creek where Howard Egan was waiting with the westbound mail. It totaled about 300 letters from the east, an accumulation during the suspended service. A cheering sight for Roberts was a detachment of U. S. troops under Lieutenant Perkins which had traveled with Egan. When the two divisions' bosses had exchanged the mail and said their goodbyes, 50 of the soldiers continued on with Roberts' group back to Carson City.

They arrived safely on June 22nd and the delayed mail was sent on to San Francisco, where it was received June 25th—the first Pony mail in three weeks.

Now, a strange thing happened. In the face of threatened disintegration across Nevada, Russell heaped another wager on the political gambling table. Coincident with the delayed mail's arrival at Carson City, it was announced that trips thereafter would be dispatched twice as often, or semiweekly, on Wednesdays and Saturdays, from both ends of the line.

A rumor about semiweekly trips had circulated in California around the middle of May. Later that same month in Washington the Senate was scheduled to take up the ill-fated Overland Mail Bill, authored by Senator Hale. Russell had lobbied long and hard for his interest in the measure. At this critical juncture a doubling of the Pony's timetable would further dramatize the Central Route and might well influence the outcome. Plainly, the bold maneuver was Russell's last-ditch effort.

Instructions to carry out the plan had little sympathy for the crippled line in Nevada, although there is room to speculate that, at the time of issuing them, Russell may not have been aware of the Indian uprising. The order seems to have been delivered by the last westbound rider to slip through the roving Indian bands before Finney, on June 1st, halted further trips. The rider reached Carson City that same day, and was the only means of conveying word to Howard Egan and Finney for simultaneous re-opening of the route.

Public advertisements of the improved scheduling were carried in California newspapers soon after July 1st. The editorial reaction, of course, was elated, although publishers as yet had hardly become accustomed to once-a-week Pony mail.

But there proved to be more in the doing than the saying. After Bolivar Roberts checked in at Carson City with his soldier escort, one more Pony trip came through, arriving at San Francisco, via river steamer, on July 1st. Then there was silence. For two long weeks Californians waited for the promised semi-weekly express. Butterfield Overland Mail coaches pulling into San Francisco carried word that the couriers had been leaving the eastern end on the new schedule. Yet none was getting through. Charitably, the friendly *Alta* concluded that the route had not been restocked.

Actually, it was the same old trouble—Indians. The big rush to institute semiweekly departures simply failed to consider the redskin problem. Winnemucca's Pah-Utes may have been whipped, but the Gosh-Utes and other tribes of the Shoshone nation were still on the rampage east of Washoe. Finally, in the middle of July, a rider reached Carson City. From there Finney testily explained the difficulty in a telegram to the impatient press. "There was no reason to expect the Pony more than one day earlier than it came," he remonstrated. "The express had to travel 200 miles with an escort and this, of course, detained it."

By now Russell's gamble had failed, the Hale bill having run aground in the House. Senator Gwin had fought the proposal—a Republican measure—at every turn. He had what was termed the "most positive assurance" from the administration that, after adjournment of Congress, the Post Office would increase the schedule of stagecoach mail on the Central Route to semiweekly trips. Postmaster General Holt, however, reneged on the promise, if it was that, and ordered a contract drawn for transport by ocean steamer.

Perhaps half expecting chicanery, the wily Senator had played one more ace from his politician's sleeve. Just before Congress went home, Gwin introduced a bill that was a sort of consolation prize for Russell. It authorized a subsidy for the Pony Express on the Central Route, something it had never had. The sum of $2,000 per month was to be paid for weekly service, or $3,000 per month for semiweekly service, plus the right of pre-empting quarter-sections of land for each 20 miles of route.

This peanut-size proposal got exactly nowhere, sped in that direction by Russell himself. Haughtily, he asserted that the Pony would continue to run with or without government aid— an obvious disclaimer of his gambling motive.

Chapter Eight

MEN WITH THE REINS

EVERYWHERE across the endless prairieland that stretched westward from the Missouri River, Russell, Majors & Waddell was a name to be reckoned with, signifying the biggest, most powerful outfit in overland freighting. From 1855 when Majors, newly successful in Army hauling, joined forces with Russell and Waddell, their long trains of lumbering bull wagons snaked over the plains with a virtual monopoly in military haulage. The roads leading to Army posts along the Santa Fe Trail and to garrisons as far west as Salt Lake City became rutted by the wheels of as many as 500 of their deep-sided wooden wagons, lumbering behind teams of cattle totaling 7,500 head. About 1,700 employees were on their payroll.

By comparison the lustrous Pony Express, as a business enterprise, was a minor sideline which, save for its romance and adventure, might conveniently have been forgotten as an embarrassing financial flop. But, paradoxically, the profitless Pony —not the lucrative freight wagons—earned the partners their collective niche in the historical hall of fame.

They gave life to the racing courser and lent it the flavor and perspective of their own characters. In consequence, much of the Pony's story is best told in the lives of these men, and of those who acted as their lieutenants along the trail.

WILLIAM HEPBURN RUSSELL—This prime mover of the horse express was born January 31, 1812, the son of William Eaton and Myrtilla Russell of Burlington, Vermont, where the father had settled after emigrating from England. About a century before, an ancestor, Lord William Russell, was beheaded for plotting against Charles II. The child never knew his father; he died while soldiering in the War of 1812. Soon after, the widow married Oliver Bangs, and under the wing of this new head of the house the family moved to Missouri in the 1820's.

There, in the town of Liberty, young Russell, reaching the age of 16, found employment as a clerk in the store of Ely & Curtis. Three years later he switched jobs and went to work in Robert Aull's store. In time, Aull, a prominent retail chain merchant, was to become a partner and financial backer in some of Russell's ventures.

At the glowing peak of his fame, built on a galaxy of promotional enterprises spanning the continent, Russell had become a national figure in commerce and politics. His interests and investments lay wherever instinct and judgment pointed to money-making possibilities. Retail merchandising, banking, cattle brokerage, warehousing, railroading, land speculation—like an industrious bee he touched them all.

At the age of 25 he formed a partnership to open a store under the name of Allen, Russell & Co., and later, with James H. Bullard, opened a second one as Bullard & Russell. Bankruptcy of the latter firm dampened neither his ingenuity nor enthusiasm, for he continued to buy more shares in the Lexington (Missouri) First Addition Company, which he helped organize, until he held controlling interest. Meanwhile, he built a 20-room mansion, and took up 3,000 acres of government land in Lafayette and Ray Counties, Missouri.

Sandwiched between these dealings he accepted a four-year term as Lexington postmaster, and took on the job as county treasurer. With several years of profitable hauling under his belt as a freighter of government supplies, he helped, in 1853, to promote the Lexington and Boonville Railroad Company, and in the following year the Lexington and Davis County Railroad.

By the time he was 36, an associate in one of Russell's ventures characterized him as "generally too sanguine," a complaint, evidently, that his optimism tended to recklessness. In retrospect, it seems to have stemmed from a supreme self-confidence, bordering on egotism. Early in life he had developed a keen appreciation of the arithmetic involved in a business deal, counterbalancing it with a gambler's instinct for a good speculation.

He was, in effect, a born opportunist, a chance-taker, an entrepreneur—one of that breed whose propensity for lone-wolf free wheeling is fair assurance that there will be misunderstanding and argument. In full measure he suffered both, whether over such ill-considered risks as the Leavenworth & Pikes Peak Express, his maneuvering with government officials, or his commitment in Washington to establish the Pony without bothering to check with his partners.

Personally, Russell was genteel in manner—but quick to anger when his judgment was challenged—and somewhat of a dandy in dress. He held himself aloof from the rough ways and habits of the boisterous frontier where he was raised, and his hands never knew the feel of a bullwhacker's rawhide nor a farmer's plow. Rather, he relied on brainpower to earn his way. Not until he passed on the Pony's reins of leadership—then nearly at the age of 50—did he feel the magic pull of the expanding West. Stronger by far was the pull of established city life and its comforts, society and opportunities.

ALEXANDER MAJORS — By upbringing, education and character, the second member of the trinity of partners was as unlike Russell as the common dandelion is to the cultivated rose. An earthy, homespun product of a farm, Majors was born October 4, 1814, in Simpson County, Kentucky, of plain, honest toilers of the soil. Beil Kelly, his maternal grandfather, seems to have been his most notable ancestor. That family-honored Irishman was a soldier in the ranks of General Washington when the redoubtable Cornwallis surrendered.

In 1818, his father, Benjamin Majors, loaded his wife, Laurania, and three children into a prairie schooner and headed westward to find new land in the rich soil of western Missouri, on the sparsely settled fringe of the great frontier. At the Fort Osage Military Reservation, near where the Missouri River bends eastward, he pulled up and pointed to a low rise in the land that would be the family's homesite. Benjamin erected a crude, one-window cabin and life began anew.

That is to say, the uneventful daily toil of plowing, seeding, cultivating, harvesting, sewing, canning resumed. The next year Laurania died from an injury sustained in an accident on the trip from Kentucky. Young Alex pitched in, helping his father in the countless farm chores. As a lad of 13 it was noted he had become a tolerably good farmhand, equally capable on the business end of plow or scythe.

The great school of the frontier offered little chance for formal book l'arnin', and it has been related (and refuted) that Majors did not learn to read until he had attained adulthood. In any event, he had scant education in the academic sense. Spiritually, it was different. From parental teaching and the exhortations of itinerant preachers he acquired puritanical views on religion, buttressed by rigorous moral and spiritual convictions. Early in his freighting experiments he surprised his employees by adopting the unheard of practice of observing the Sabbath as a day of rest, even when on the open trail. Moreover, believing it would inure to their safety and dignity, he presented each of them with a small Bible.

In 1834, now 20 years old, Majors married Catherine Stalcup from a nearby farm, and erected a home for his bride on land which his father gave from the family homestead. Restless and ambitious, he found time, between raising crops of farm and family, to add to his income by hauling produce of neighboring farms to Independence, and to trade with the Indians across the Missouri River. He owned a fine team of oxen and became reputed as the best bullwhacker in the settlement.

So it was a rather natural consequence that, after several years of having watched wagon trains rattle out of Independence and head out along the Santa Fe Trail, Majors should conclude that this was a business for him. To his experienced eye there were flaws in the way trains were organized and how the teams were handled. With a local wainwright he contracted to have his one wagon refurbished, bought five more, partially on credit, and purchased 78 head of oxen. He persuaded merchants in Independence and at Westport Landing to trust him with consignments, and loaded one wagon with products of his own farm.

Thus, on August 10, 1848, Majors, the farmer, became Majors, the overland freighter. From Westport Landing, site of future Kansas City, his oxen strained into their yokes, wagon wheels creaked, and the little train, forerunner of giant caravans, began its interminable trek to Santa Fe. Sixteen hundred miles and 92 days later he was back, acclaimed for setting a new round-trip record. After paying off his teamsters and the money owing on his wagons, it was said there was $1,500 left—a tidy three-months' profit.

In 1853, when he returned from hauling military supplies to Fort Union, following an earlier trip the same year to Santa Fe, he was a rich man. The intervening years had been good. Six wagons had increased to 10, then 25. Both civilian and military ladings had filled his jouncing bottoms and his reputation for reliability was firmly established.

Having had a taste of government hauling, he wanted more. In December he entered a bid at Fort Leavenworth with Major E. A. Ogden, quartermaster for the military posts west of the Missouri, for the next year's contract, and won it. He probably outbid Russell, for the great promoter was without a government contract in 1854, being reduced to a single train of civilian goods, dispatched to California. The venture turned out to be a poor substitute, as Russell lost about 20 per cent of his cattle along the way.

'Fifty-four was Majors' biggest year in sole proprietorship. He put 100 wagons and 1,200 oxen on the trail. The sight of his long duck-covered caravans must have put sand in the craw of the prominent and successful Russell, who himself had rolled as many as 135 wagons in a twelvemonth. The volatile, temperamental promoter likely saw little justice or logic in this strong challenge from a once small-time operator.

But the truth was Alexander Majors had arrived. He was a formidable competitor, whether anybody liked it or not.

In November, when Majors returned from the plains, Russell had a plan. West of the Missouri River military posts and their soldier complements had rapidly multiplied, as protection for increasing numbers of overland emigrants became a more pressing problem of the government. Freighting contracts, let on competitive bids, until now had sufficed to supply the Army. Now it was apparent that the vast ladings to be carried could no longer depend on the wagons, cattle and men which a single bidder could hastily gather in advance. Hauling for the military had become big business. So it was determined that Major Ogden at Fort Leavenworth would negotiate a contract on the basis of a freighter's financial ability and experience.

Russell, associated with Waddell, put the proposition up to Majors. Together, pooling their resources, they could hold a monopoly on military freighting everywhere west of the Big Muddy. The contract to be let in '55 would run two years.

Majors agreed, influenced, perhaps, by Russell's unique proposal to establish a new, lucrative set of charges. Henceforth, there would be a flat rate per hundredweight per hundred miles of travel, instead of a single charge per hundred pounds to destination. On December 28, 1854, the three men formally signed a partnership contract. Two years later they were to show a profit of $300,000—more money than freighting had earned any of them before.

WILLIAM BRADFORD WADDELL—Someone once said that Russell had the brains, Majors the money, and Waddell the name—whatever that meant. Of the three, Waddell, man and name, is the least known. His anonymity is not assignable to history writers, for this third member of the firm was seldom in the limelight of the more spectacular aspects of the business —the financial gymnastics, or the driving of ox teams. While the enterprising Russell busied himself on prolonged jaunts to New York and Washington, buttonholing bankers and lobbying Congress, and while the intrepid Majors was plodding across the wilderness with an endless line of canopied conestogas, William B. Waddell stayed at home, the watchdog of the exchequer and manager of the day-to-day trivia that required proprietary decision.

It was a fair assignment. He was a successful merchant, accustomed to the management of inventories and the purchase of staples and equipment. As such he was familiar with going prices and sources of supply for the long list of items needed to outfit and sustain an overland train.

Like Majors, Waddell as a lad had lived on a Kentucky farm, his father having brought the family there from Virginia. With the wanderlust of youth, at 17, he struck out for fortune and adventure, trying his hand as a lead miner at Galena, Illinois, a store clerk in bustling St. Louis, then back home, as a farmer once more. Marriage in 1834, accompanied by a handsome dowry, enabled him to leave farm life for good, and he

ST. LOUIS AND LEAVENWORTH TELEGRAPH—STEBBINS LINE.

This Line is now, and will be kept in constant working order, and in connection with other Lines to all parts of the country. Our patrons are requested to report to me, at the earliest moment, by letter to St. Louis, Mo., any cause of dissatisfaction, and it shall be promptly remedied. We pay Operators liberally, and intend to make them do their duty. In this our patrons are equally interested, and they should aid us accordingly.

We will not be responsible for dispatches beyond our own line; but in case of delays or mistakes on our line, will promptly refund the amount paid us and no more; except when to insure the correctness of a dispatch we receive fifty per cent. in addition to the regular tariff for repeating the dispatch back; and in that case we will be responsible for actual damage only, to an amount not exceeding one hundred times the amount paid us for the dispatch.

CHARLES M. STEBBINS, President.

SEND THE FOLLOWING MESSAGE SUBJECT TO THE ABOVE CONDITIONS:

Washington 6th 1860

To Waddell Jones & Majors

Ficklin dispatches today following: "Your two letters to Roberson received — Send a man for my place and that damned quick." Letters referred to on subject of Circular — Put Clute in charge at once — Full particulars by mail

Wm H Russell

Paid

Benjamin F. Ficklin, the self-willed superintendent of the Pony Express line, who "told off" President Russell in a hotly-worded telegram, and the subsequent wire from Russell ordering his discharge.

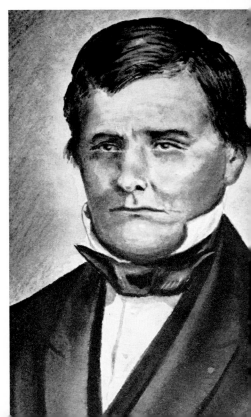

The founders and first proprietors of the Pony Express: upper left, William H. Russell; upper right, Alexander Majors; and William B. Waddell. Original drawings by Reg Emerson, from old photograph reproductions.

turned to storekeeping, in Mayslick, Kentucky. In something like three years, hearing of richer possibilities on the frontier, he sold out, packed up, and moved to Lexington, Missouri.

Lexington was one of the leading towns in the state, the largest on the frontier. Opening a store on the river front, Waddell prospered commercially as a businessman and socially as a respected citizen.

His business, retailing and wholesaling of produce, hemp and grain, was profitable, enabling him, like Russell, to become interested in locally-founded insurance and banking enterprises. Their paths ran parallel in other matters. Both attended the same Baptist church and lived in the same neighborhood— as a matter of fact, across the street from one another in equally pretentious homes. The two joined as partners in Waddell, Ramsey & Co. for the manufacture of rope and bags, and also in the merchandising firm of Morehead, Waddell & Co., which later became Waddell & Russell. It was the latter company, first dabbling in overland freighting in 1853, that eventually merged with Majors.

The three men were a study in contrast, yet each was a sort of counterbalance for the other. Russell, chief promoter and head salesman, a *bon vivant* Beau Brummell, was the bold plunger, confident, temperamental, the very antithesis of Majors. Here was the honest, simple, straightforward man of the soil whose intimate, practical experience with man and beast made him the inevitable choice to oversee the sweat and dust and toil along the trail.

That left Waddell the only job open. Slow and ponderous in his middle age, a calculating thinker, disposed to bickering, but keen of judgment and cool in reasoning—ever the practical businessman—the tending of the homefires, where he could do the most good and the least harm, was his obvious assignment.

Of the five division superintendents hired to supervise the company route, Joseph A. "Jack" Slade, roughhouse whiskey

drinker and uninhibited gun-slinger, easily pre-empts attention.
Alternately a man of courteous manner and a merciless killer,
he seemingly escaped the notice of Majors' principled eye when
he was taken on by the company as a carry-over from the
stumbling Hockaday line. From Fort Kearny to Horseshoe Station, where he lived in unexplained luxury with a sour-coun-
tenanced, heavy-haunched wife, Slade ran a tight, fear-struck
division, exercising ruthless control with a quickly-riled temper
and a ready gun. But his chameleon character was disarming.
Mark Twain, quite aware of his awful history, found him "a
pleasant person, friendly and gentle-spoken."

At an immigrant ford on the South Platte, called the California Crossing, the company had established a station to serve
the stages it had bought from Hockaday. A Frenchman, named
Jules Reni, who had previously settled there and was conduct-
ing a profitable trade with travelers, was appointed station
keeper, and the place came to be known as Julesburg.

Jules was a man of innately vile character and his ethics
in business belied him not. Lying, cheating and *caveat emptor*
were his accustomed tools of trade. Horses which he swapped
to immigrants often found their way back to his corral in the
dead of night, and goods that he sold were robbed from the
buyer to be sold again. His iniquity, compounded with fraud
in company affairs, was discovered by Benjamin Ficklin while
traveling through on an inspection trip. He ordered Slade to
replace the rogue and arrange with him a settlement on missing
company property.

That idea didn't appeal to Jules. When Slade appeared to
carry out his instructions, he was met by the blast of a double-
barreled shotgun. Either Jules' aim was off or he skimped a
few shot in loading, for Slade was carried away, not quite dead,
to recuperate. On the next stage, the story goes, Ficklin arrived,
saw his duty, hanged Jules, and promptly departed again. But
cohorts of the Frenchman, in the nick of time, cut him down,
and the outlaws went into hiding.

When Slade had recovered, he returned to the scene with revenge in his heart and lead in his gun. He is said to have cornered the would-be killer at Pacific Springs. Disabling him with a ball in the thigh, he trussed him up to a corral post. Jules lived a long time as Slade moved back and deliberately used him for target practice. When it was all over, Slade drew a knife and sliced off his ears. One of them he is reported to have used as a watch fob and the other as a macabre saloon stunt, in which he casually tossed the shriveled appendage on the bar and asked for change.

Jules' killing wasn't Slade's first. As a lad of 13, in Carlisle, Illinois, he hurled a rock, killing a man who had tried to straighten out a juvenile difficulty. The parents of the morbid kid hustled him off to Texas, where he later enlisted in the Mexican War. He subsequently found a job with a freighting outfit out of St. Joseph, and is said to have killed a fellow employee and drinking companion who had made the mistake of daring him to shoot.

The man loved liquor. While in Denver, on a drunken spree, he shot up a saloon, putting a bullet into a friendly intruder who attempted to quiet him. The man happened to be David Street, an official of the Overland Mail Company, under whose auspices the Pony Express was then running. Luckily, he had received only a superficial wound and didn't fire Slade who, when he sobered up, abjectly apologized.

At Fort Halleck there was another spree, another shooting, which left the sutler's store in shambles. This time there was no saving him, when the angry commandant flatly insisted on his being discharged.

The final days of this legendary miscreant were spent in the tumultuous, lawless mining town of Virginia City, Montana. Here again drink was his undoing, as was his old hobby of shooting up the place of imbibing. At first he was supposed to have had money to pay for damages, but when that ran out stern measures were in order. From a miners' court, established by a vigilantes' committee, came a warrant for his arrest. Defiantly, he tore it into shreds. It was the last straw. The vigilantes caught him, still drunk, and strung him up.

Bolivar Roberts, division superintendent at Carson City, was cut from a distinctly different mold. Although, like Slade, he was left largely on his own responsibility, his record is lily white in matters of debauchery and wickedness. Instead, a measure of his quality is shown in his personal bravery as leader of a handful of men, traveling the dangerous Indian-infested trail to meet Howard Egan with the mail.

A native of Winchester, Stark County, Illinois, he left home as a youth of 19 and migrated to the Utah Territory. His father, Dr. Daniel Roberts, joined him the next year, 1851, and with Bolivar's four brothers, they settled in Provo, Utah. It proved to be but a temporary abode, for in 1852 Dr. Roberts took two of his sons, Bolivar and William, to Placerville where he resumed his practice of medicine and the boys took up mining.

The following eight years of Bolivar Roberts' life, up to the start of the Pony Express, are unknown. A tiny crossing, established on the Carson River, called the Bolivar Roberts Toll Bridge, leads to the assumption that he crossed the Sierras with other Washoe hopefuls and built the bridge to serve traffic between the mines. Its exact location has been forgotten, but it possibly played a part in his selection as an agent of the Pony Express, the proprietors of which used existing facilities wherever they could.

Due to the proximity of General Agent Finney, who exercised primary supervision over the full western section, Roberts' authority and scope of duty were more limited than other division superintendents on the route. Carson City, where he headquartered, was only a tiny mining community and his barren segment of the Pony trail east of there necessarily had to depend on Finney in California for supplies, provisions and livestock replacement. But he was not a mere station keeper or agent; another man performed that work. His duties were concerned with the physical aspects of the operation, the care of men and stock which Finney supplied.

When the express came to an end, Roberts took up mining in Virginia City, Nevada, then in Wyoming, and later near Salt Lake City. After 1871, in the latter place, he farmed, raised stock and opened a drug store which his son managed. By 1888, when 57, he was described as a "man of considerable means."

Benjamin F. Ficklin, route superintendent, or general manager, of Russell, Majors & Waddell's stage and Pony Express operations, was a highly controversial figure in the organization and he enjoyed but a short tenure on the payroll. He first appeared as a member of the Leavenworth & Pikes Peak Express Company which he helped Russell and others organize in February, 1859. Nine months later, when the company was reorganized as the Central Overland California & Pikes Peak Express Company, he was listed as one of the incorporators, but evidently subscribed to none of the 5,000 shares of $100 capital stock.

Clearly Ficklin was a man of great personal ambitions, with a strong will to bring them to reality. His projection from an obscure frontiersman in Utah into the limelight of big-time freighting as a colleague of the largest operators in the whole West was, in just a year's time, no mean accomplishment. And William H. Russell, who was to become his chief critic, held that he was out to make the most of it.

From the outset both Waddell and Majors were vigorously opposed to the Pony Express which they felt, rightly, would undermine the firm's already shaky financial condition. As partners of Russell, though, they were obliged to accede to the plan when he anounced that, in Washington, he had pledged the word of the company. Ficklin, on the other hand, was jubilant; he wasn't sobered by the thought of his own money being put to risk. When the first trip was completed and the Pony Express proved to be a practical idea, his enthusiasm was boundless.

About 45 days after commencement of the service, he journeyed to Washington and proposed to Russell that the schedule be doubled, from weekly to semiweekly. His timing for the suggestion was most inopportune. Only five trips had been dispatched from either end of the line, and its success, in terms of mail volume handled, was yet to be established. Russell, meanwhile, was being stretched on the rack of his own arithmetic. Not yet had he secured the long-coveted mail contract which would assure continued and substantial income. Until that happy day he was faced with the grim task of raising large sums of money to keep the insolvent stage and express lines afloat. Economy was the watchword.

Ficklin got nowhere with his plan and returned to the West. Afterward, when it served his own purpose as we have seen, Russell readily adopted the idea and put it into effect. The meeting had served only to fan a smouldering feud between them. Russell, constantly under the financial gun, had little faith in the brand of economy as practiced in the field by Ficklin. The route superintendent contended that his management was capable, and both Waddell and Majors supported him.

Shortly after Ficklin departed, Russell penned some derogatory statements about him to Joseph Roberson of the firm's St. Joseph office. Ficklin chanced to read them and fired a telegram to Russell: "Send a man for my place damned quick."

Angered and unappreciative of the rudeness, Russell took him at his word and told his partners to put J. H. Clute in the job. The feud now blazed merrily. Russell's instructions were ignored, so he asked for a board of directors meeting, to take Ficklin's resignation. Waddell said no, for the company couldn't get along without him. To this Russell replied that it was either Ficklin or himself, and in the latter event would his partners please arrange to sell his stock?

The ultimatum shocked them. Waddell got Ficklin to write a letter of apology, and he was relieved of duty pending a reaction to a conciliatory telegram hastily sent off by Waddell.

But the maneuver didn't work. "I cannot, will not," Russell hotly replied, "consent to his again taking charge as superintendent. He is too self-willed . . . As for economy he knows it not, and not only so, he has nothing to lose in the way of money. His only desire seems to be to get up a big name (at our expense) for a splendid line . . . he would circumvent me if possible, blow the whole thing to gratify his unlawful ambition to rule or ruin."

There was no mollifying him, even when Waddell wrote that Russell was just like Ficklin—that he "must ride the lead horse or not go at all"—and so the two should adjust their differences and compose themselves. Back came Russell's retort that he'd rather see the whole enterprise sunk, together with his own prospects, than to go on with the dispute.

About the first of July Ficklin's resignation was accepted.

Seemingly, his year of hobnobbing with the transportation greats of the West entitled the ex-route boss to consider himself as having "arrived." Shortly afterwards, he was in Washington, dickering, with other bidders, to build the government-subsidized overland telegraph. Ficklin proposed to run a pony express between the ends of the wires, to be strung from east and west, eliminating the express service of his former colleagues.

The Treasury Department awarded the contract to a group headed by Hiram Sibley. Actually, Ficklin, as well as two other contenders, had markedly underbid Sibley for the government concession, but oddly enough they all withdrew when it came time to give bond for fulfillment of the contract. Sibley was appreciative. When the Pacific Telegraph Company was incorporated in Nebraska June 11, 1861, Ficklin was shown as one of the incorporators.

By then, however, the drums of Civil War were beating and he had gone to Virginia. There a rebel legislature, on April 21, 1861, adopted an ordinance, instructing Governor John Letcher to commission him a major in charge of the quartermaster department, ordnance, of the state's Confederate forces.

When the great fratricide ended, Ficklin found his way back to his first love, the mail service. In 1867, in association with Frederick P. Sawyer, he won a weekly mail contract between San Antonio, Texas, and Fort Smith, Arkansas. The latter place had been a principal division point on the line of an old competitor, the Butterfield Overland Mail.

Ultimately, the southwest requited Ficklin's greatest ambitions. Here he was prominently successful as a stageman, became wealthy, and, as Russell put it, "got a big name" for himself. Surely he took pride in a little townsite near Fort Concho, present-day San Angelo. Surely he grieved its loss when it was washed out in the Concho River flood of August, 1882. The town's name? Ben Ficklin.

In detailing establishment of the Pony Express, writers have described William W. Finney as "just the man" to organize the western end of the line. The label is a bit puzzling, for of all the route managers employed by the Pony he is the least known. Without fanfare, announcement or explanation, he simply appeared at the beginning, having journeyed by sea from New York to make the necessary arrangements on the Pacific Coast, and six months later departed without so much as a fond ado. Who he was, where he went, and what he became are mysteries for the biographical delver.

Only the short span of his stewardship as General Agent of the Pacific provides a clue to the man. Full credit is his for organizing the route, single-handedly, all the way west from Roberts Creek, Nevada, a stretch of some 400 miles. On his shoulders alone rested the responsibility of locating suitable relay points, hiring men, buying stock and feed, laying in supplies of grub and equipment, and soliciting business.

According to the Pony's signed newspaper ads, it wasn't until after the middle of April, when the first two eastward trips had been dispatched, that he engaged Joseph Lambert, San Francisco agent for the Alta Telegraph Company, to act as the local Pony Express representative. Neither, until then, had he taken on John W. Coleman as agent in Sacramento, or P. Lovell at Carson City.

Obviously, he was a man of resourceful initiative. How much easier it would have been, in the face of the frightful Pah-Ute attacks, to close up shop and await the outcome of the fighting. He must have had to swallow a choking lump of company and personal pride to wire Sacramento for public financial aid. Not that he was unaccustomed to a shortage of money. Earlier, when his operating funds had given out, he had gone to Ben Holladay in San Francisco and persuaded him to accept drafts for operating capital. Holladay was there on the persuasion of Finney's boss in an entirely different venture. Finney probably called on him at the Sacramento and Leidesdorff Street office of Holladay & Russell, brokers of "riding, work and pack" mules for travelers to the Washoe mines.

It seems incongruous, then, that this man of get-up-and-go, this successful persuader, would allow himself to be maneuvered into a public argument with important patrons of the Pony Express. As a service to the community, newspapers in San Francisco had taken it upon themselves to post an advance list of Pony mail addressees, received by wire from Carson City. The posting enabled commercial houses to learn of incoming letters more than 24 hours ahead of delivery, an obvious advantage when expected letters entailed shipping advices, rates of exchange and other money matters.

Finney ordered the papers to cease the practice, whereupon, on the sixth of September, 11 of the leading businessmen in San Francisco circulated a round robin to the General Agent, outlining the conveniences of the prior notices and asking that they be reinstated. The protest was sent off to him at Sacramento, and a copy to a local newspaper. Finney summarily rejected it without giving his reasons. The paper proceeded to publish the complaint for the whole town to read.

Thirteen days later William W. Finney was no longer the General Agent of the Pacific. W. C. Marley, formerly keeper of Buckland's Station, returned from entirely restocking the western division of the route and announced that he had accepted appointment to the job. Finney simply faded from the picture.

Marley seems to have remained on the job until the clatter of the Pony's hooves was silenced by the click of the telegraph key. One month later, Governor James W. Nye appointed him sheriff of Nevada Territory. The position, he knew, was no sinecure. Only a few days previously Sheriff John L. Blackburn was murdered in Carson City, the victim of an irate gambler's slashing knife.

Chapter Nine

MEN ON THE TRAIL

While I am in the employ of A. Majors, I agree not to use profane language, not to get drunk, not to gamble, not to treat animals cruelly, and not to do anything else that is incompatible with the conduct of a gentleman. And I agree, if I violate any of the above conditions, to accept my discharge without any pay for my services.

No ONE WENT to work for Majors—or later for Russell, Majors & Waddell, where he insisted that his hiring practices be adopted—without signing this pledge against sin. When he first embarked upon the plains the confirmed moralist was aghast at the vulgarity and profanity that was prevalent in the trains, and vowed he'd have none of these "daring, rough men" to contend with or to offend his high principles. It wasn't that he claimed to be holier than thou. Contemporary middle-class thought, inculcated and molded on the frontier by traveling evangelicals and illiberal Protestantism, tended to be prudish. It was a sort of immunization from the Jacksonian common man, who, freed now from the shackles of caste, was apt to comport himself with crude indignity.

To Major's mind the unique contract produced the desired results, for, whether through naivete or honest recollection, years later as an octogenarian he couldn't remember that a single man had been discharged without pay. Rather, he observed, "I can state with truthfulness that never in the history of freighting on the plains did such quiet, gentlemanly, fraternal feelings exist among men who were in my employ and governed by these rules."

So mote it be. But there is an entertainingly different view, offered by the English author and traveler, Sir Richard Burton who, in 1860, journeyed the full length of the Pony Express trail and stopped at most of the stations.

"His meritorious efforts to reform the morals of the land have not yet put forth even the bud of promise," Sir Richard caustically noted of Majors' proselyting. "He forbad his drivers and employees to drink, gamble, curse, and travel on Sundays; he desired them to peruse Bibles, distributed to them gratis; and though he refrained from a lengthy proclamation commanding his lieges to be good boys and girls he did not the less expect it of them. Results: I scarcely ever saw a sober driver; as for profanity—the western equivalent for hard swearing— they would make the blush of shame crimson the cheek of the old Isis bargee; and, rare exceptions to the rule of the United States, they are not to be deterred from evil talking even by the dread presence of a 'lady'."

Somewhere between these opposite poles of literary license perhaps may be divined a less apocryphal idea of the real character and daily life of the men along the Pony trail. One of them, at least, would rise from the dead to defend the stimulating effect of Majors' campaign against moral turpitude. Zealously scrawled across the flyleaf of his Bible was this oath to self-betterment:

Kauble will not hereafter during his Life, drink any Strong drink Such as Spiritual liquor From this day hensforth now and Forever.   F. M. Kauble

How assiduously Pony Express employees embraced the tenets of their four-by-six-inch calf-bound Bibles or to what extent their Sundays were devoted to the holy precepts, as was Majors' implied wish, is a question of ruminating interest. So far as is known, appeals to the Almighty for help in times of travail have gone unrecorded in the numerous anecdotes and legends of riders and station keepers. Indeed, there is but a single instance of the Deity's name being called, and that was the startled ejaculation, "My God, Wood, it's Indians!"

The cry was uttered at the height of the savage Ute attacks in Nevada. Albert Armstrong and Henry Woodville Wilson were keepers of the Pony station at Egan Canyon. Their shelter was a warm, one-room log cabin, equipped with a camping outfit, plenty of provisions, ammunition and a few books.

One morning after finishing breakfast, Armstrong heard a "low, weird, moaning" outside the cabin and, peeking out the calico curtain, involuntarily cried his "my God" warning to Wilson. The sight chilled him to the marrow of his bones. Outside were not just a few idle Indian wanderers who commonly visited Pony stations, but a full threatening band, ominously bedecked in war paint and feathers and stripped naked except for loin cloths. Their skins were greased and glistened in the bright sun.

The intruders carried no firearms, a discovery that gave the keepers only small hope. Grabbing their rifles, they fell prone to the floor and commenced firing through cracks in the mortared wall. But ammunition was not plentiful and soon their last ball was fired. The Indians sensed the situation and burst through the door with a terrifying shriek. Before the attackers could lay hands on Armstrong and Wilson the chief was at the doorway, standing with folded arms, and lordly commanding that the two men bring forth their bread. This they obliged in good quantity and on further orders proceeded to bake an extraordinary number of loaves from a plentiful stock of the station's flour.

The savages set to and gorged themselves, while their two prisoners sat fitfully on the floor, shaken by terrible thoughts of their possible fate. Eventually it was made known. The two keepers would die at sundown—by burning at the stake. In due time the savages began a great preparation in the station yard. A wagon tongue was detached and driven solidly into the ground for a stake. Other Indians gathered sagebrush and heaped it in a circle.

Inside, a massive petrifying fear settled over Armstrong and Wilson as they abjectly gave up all hope of somehow evading a horrible, gruesome death. Then, miraculously, they heard a rush of pounding hooves from the direction of a nearby hill. That welcome sound could mean only one thing—rescue. Outside there ensued a maelstrom of cracking rifles, the surprised cries of Indians, mixed with the staccato of galloping horses.

Colonel E. J. Steptoe, with a passing contingent of U. S. cavalrymen, had luckily seen the strange goings on in the station yard. His charge quickly stampeded the Indians, several of whom were killed in the chase that followed. Enough got away, however, to raid the Shell Creek station that same night, killing the three keepers and stealing their horses.

For many employees, narrow escapes, bravery and hardship seemingly comprised a way of life. Their trail is amply strewn with heroic tales of bold daring and intrepid feats. Which of the episodes are solid fact and which are salted narratives is of diminishing importance (however annoying be the bewilderment) in a century of lengthening perspective, for together fact and legend adequately limn the background of the Pony's eventful time.

There are, for example, the conflicting accounts of several riders, each claiming the distinction of having spurred his mount on the longest ride. Jack Keetley, a lad of 19 or 20, rode on A. E. Lewis' division between St. Joseph and Fort Kearny. He was one of the few riders whose tenure ran as long as the

Pony, and during his time had carried the mail between all stations on the division. For some reason not well explained—one version relates it was on a wager—Keetley jumped into his saddle at Big Sandy Station in Nebraska Territory and toted the *mochila* all the way to Elwood, Kansas, across the river from St. Joe; then doubled back with the westbound mail, which he relinquished at Seneca, Kansas. His continuous ride reportedly took 31 hours. Superintendent Lewis, apparently doubtful of the claim, clocked the distance with a "roadometer" attached to his buggy wheel and alleged that it was 340 miles.

This rider's remarkable resistance to fatigue, however, seems to have been eclipsed by another's trip made under more harrowing circumstances. The hero involved was Robert "Pony Bob" Haslam, whose name is synonymous with Pony Express in factual and fictional history. His most noteworthy event in horsemanship occurred in May, 1860. At Friday's Station, at the southern tip of Lake Bigler (Lake Tahoe), he received the eastbound *mochila,* containing what was probably the May 10th mail from San Francisco, and dashed off for Buckland's Station, a distance of about 75 miles. It was several days after the raid on Williams' Station and, therefore, reasonable to assume that he was aware of the danger ahead.

His first confirmation came at Reed's Station, east of Carson City, where he found that the citizen's army had commandeered the relay mounts to pursue Winnemucca. He halted long enough to feed his horse, then spurred on to Buckland's.

Johnny Richardson, his relief rider, suffered from chattering knees, badly frightened over the Indian threat. He refused to take the mail. W. C. Marley, the station keeper, offered a bonus of $50 to Haslam if he would carry on instead. Pony Bob replied, "I'll go you once." How Marley, a mere employee himself, acquired the authority, much less the money, for such an offer isn't revealed in Haslam's account; anyhow, it sent the heroic mercenary on his way.

At Sand Springs, 35 miles eastward, he changed horses, and at Cold Springs, 34 miles further, swapped again. Smith's Creek was 30 miles beyond and reaching it he was finally relieved by Jay G. Kelley. All told, Pony Bob had raced 190 miles without rest, which he now proceeded to take.

Nine hours later he was in the saddle again, retracing his journey with the westbound mail. At Cold Springs he found a catastrophe. The horse he had left there had disappeared, so had all the other stock. In the brief interim since his eastward trip the Indians had raided the place and killed the keeper. He pressed on to Sand Springs where, with an intuitive fear of danger at this isolated spot, persuaded Montgomery Maze, the keeper, to leave the station and accompany him with the mail as far as the Sink of the Carson. There they found some 15 well-armed men, resting at the substantial adobe cabin en route home from the chase of Winnemucca.

Back at Buckland's, Haslam related his experiences to Marley who, the rider said, magnanimously boosted his bonus to $100. Taking a short nap, he again took the *mochila* and galloped over his regular run, across Carson Valley and up the mountain to Friday's Station. Altogether this single horseman had ridden 380 miles, and the mail schedule, he recalled, had been delayed but a few hours.

The tale of the greatest feat of all, in length of ride, is rather naturally recounted in the adventures of William F. "Buffalo Bill" Cody, whose extraordinary exploits in the romantic West lost nothing in the telling as the years passed. The remarkable snowballing of his achievements is graciously explained by Arthur Chapman, who says that Cody, a deservedly popular character, "was too busy as a showman in later years to curb every enthusiastic pen that was taken up in his praise."

According to Buffalo Bill's own account, he first hired on as a Pony rider in the spring of 1860, for a 45-mile run west of Julesburg. He was 15 years old, the youngest Pony rider on the payroll. Earlier he had been employed as a mounted messenger between wagon trains of Russell, Majors & Waddell. After three months of expressing the mail, he "longed for the cool air of the mountains" and quit. The next year he was re-employed and assigned to Slade's division, on a run between Red Buttes on the North Platte and Three Crossings on the Sweetwater, a distance of 116 miles.

Riding into Three Crossings one day, he found that his relief rider had been killed the night before in a drunken row. Another man was not readily available. Cody was asked to continue with the express to the next home station, Rocky Ridge, distance 76 miles.

"It was a very bad and dangerous country, but the emergency was great and I concluded to try it," Cody asserted. "I therefore started promptly from Three Crossings without more than a moment's rest. I pushed on with the usual rapidity, entering every relay station on time, and accomplished the round trip . . . back to Red Buttes, without a single mishap, on time." The span of miles was 384. "This stands on the records as being the longest Pony Express journey ever made," he explained for clarity.

Despite occasional refuge in hyperbole, it is easily discerned that even routine life in the saddle was poorly calculated to attract applicants from the skittish or faint-hearted, or from the pampered sons of gentle birth. Wherever restless men pushed the frontier beyond the borders of established society, the vanguard was liberally comprised of uneducated, roughhewn individualists, misfit escapees from the monotony of civilization and malcontents turned adventurers. Bankers, lawyers, financiers, conservative men of mark and substance, were in small minority among the explorers of the wilderness. The demand from the unknown, uncharted West was for muscled stamina in men who had little to risk, and to whom chance and fate were synonyms of excitement and opportunity.

Which is not to gainsay the clever prowess and dauntless bravery of the Pony Express rider. The American hero, for good or bad, is made of wonderful physical stuff, and with this commodity the valiant mail courier was richly endowed. So, if we find him departing the straight and narrow, neglecting the tenets of his employer, or, as Burton put it, "enjoying the mental refreshment of abundant bad language," he is not discarding the badge of heroism, only demonstrating the capacity of character.

Montgomery Maze is a case in point. Assigned as station keeper at Sand Springs, he escaped death at the hands of the Pah-Utes, and with a small group of other employees, including C. H. Ruffin and William Hamilton (the first rider out of Sacramento and now a station agent), he marched to Cold Springs Station, where the keeper had been massacred only a few days before. There they rounded up the stray sheep belonging to the company and herded them back to Carson City. Every foot of the way was through hostile Indian territory and each bend in the trail was a potential ambush.

Generously, the *Territorial Enterprise* published an account of the perilous journey. The next day the paper carried an indignant letter, co-signed by Maze and others, denying that Hamilton, as reported, had alone proceeded to Smith's Creek and returned with the sheep. Glory at best, he seemed to say, is temporary and is to be properly distributed.

Two months later, his moment of heroism passed and forgotten, Maze, now listed as a rider, disruptively became a candidate for "discharge without any pay." At Smith's Creek, on some undisclosed difference, he got involved in a violent argument with H. Trumbo, the station keeper.

Trumbo is said to have "snapped" a pistol at him several times. On the following day the fracas resumed, but this time Maze retaliated, and fired a rifle. The ball pierced Trumbo above the hip, inflicting a dangerous wound. Later, apparently frightened at the consequences, he circulated a round robin and obtained the signatures of various people, attesting that his antagonist had provoked the attack.

Thus had Maze, and Trumbo as well, observed the pledge "not to do anything incompatible with a gentleman." But they alone were not guilty of atrocious behavior; there were other infractions of the code, where death was the recompense.

One notable example occurred July 12, 1861, at the Rock Creek Station, near the Little Blue River, almost on the Nebraska-Kansas line. David McCanles, James Wood and James Gordon all met their Maker in a violent affray that exploded over an argument, the precise subject of which in after years was long debated. This slaughter marked the beginning of a 15-year gun-slinging career for an unknown stock tender at the station, a lanky 23-year-old, named J. B. "Wild Bill" Hickok.

Another escapade was marked by the sentence of Judge John Cradlebaugh who, in 1860, presided in the Carson City court of Nevada's new territorial government. He marked the Pony Express with dubitable distinction by naming one of its riders as principal in Nevada's first legal execution. The culprit was William Carr, who had murdered one Bernard Cherry at the trouble-riven Smith's Creek Station. Back in Kansas, although the passing years had released Melville Baughn from the compulsion of his pledge, he too, came to a grisly end when his life was taken in Seneca, on the charge of murder.

The scales of moral judgment are, however, by sheer weight of numbers, preponderantly in favor of the plain, honest, duty-devoted expressman. While seated in the saddle he was neither hero nor killer (save, perhaps, for a random redskin), and on his gallant performance was built the Pony's fabulous legend. And by and large his inherent goodness led him to a useful, productive life in society in after years.

Charles Cliff, a native of Missouri, became a feed and flour merchant at St. Joseph, the same city out of which he had raced with the mail, while Theodore Rand and J. G. McCall turned to railroading. Sam and Jim Gilson, brothers, went to the Utah mines, the former discovering the mineral, gilsonite. At Bountiful, Utah, John Fisher, who had ridden Pony with his brother William, served as mayor, justice of the peace and state legislator. Rider Harry L. Roff, mistakenly identified by Alexander Majors as having carried the first mail east from Sacramento, *vice* Hamilton, found employment as an express agent in Placerville, where he accommodatingly and impartially brought tidbits of news to both rival papers, the *Mountain Democrat* and the *Daily News*. Later he found his niche as an agent, and eventually a manager, of the Home Insurance Company, where, in 1906, he supervised payment of over $3,000,000 in claims arising out of the San Francisco earthquake and fire.

Keepers of the Pony stations were not, as a group, to be classed among the bored, restless adventurers who sought a front row seat in the frontier theater of excitement. Especially in the divisions east of Salt Lake City, the typical Pony attendant was of a more settled, mature nature—if one charitably overlooks such exceptions as Jules Reni and David McCanles. Here the way was intermittently marked with small settlements and occasional farms that capably served as relay points for the passing riders.

There were the Moores at the Three Crossings Station in the valley of the Sweetwater River, respected natives of England who cut short their trek to the Mormon capital to set up an excellent and famous board for both stage drivers and express couriers.

Representing the company at Fort Bridger was the businesslike Army sutler, William Alexander Carter, who had considerately insisted his wife remain in Missouri until he had accumulated sufficient capital for a comfortable home. In April, 1860, on receipt of a letter from Russell, he wrote John S. Jones: "I have received Mr. W. H. Russell's letter appointing me Agent

Left to right, seated, are J. B. Colton, Alexander Majors, and William F. "Buffalo Bill" Cody. Standing in Napoleonic pose is Robert "Pony Bob" Haslam, and beside him is Prentiss Ingraham. This 1893 photo was taken to celebrate publication of Major's book, *Seventy Years on the Frontier,* which was backed financially by Cody. This book, edited by Cody's publicity agent Ingraham, probably contains the first mention of Buffalo Bill's having been a Pony Express rider.

Trail marker for Sand Springs Station, Nevada. The actual location of the shelter was a considerable distance beyond, near the sand dune in the background.

Ruins of Fort Churchill. One of these buildings reportedly housed the eastern end of Frederick Bee's telegraph line and was a regular stop for Pony riders.

View below is the Hastings Building, Second and J Streets, Sacramento, 1855. After Wells, Fargo & Co. moved out, the Alta Telegraph occupied a storeroom in that corner of the building and functioned as local agent of the Pony Express until the spring of 1861. The picture above shows the same building today, with bearded man resting in old Pony Express doorway.

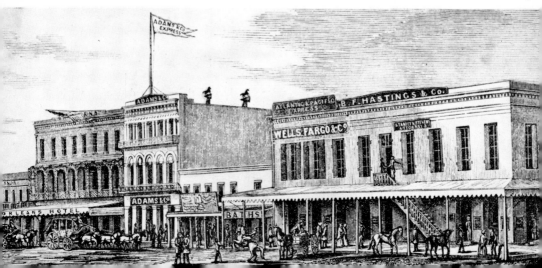

The Pony Express passes a crew of pole setters building the overland telegraph. From a painting by George M. Ottinger.

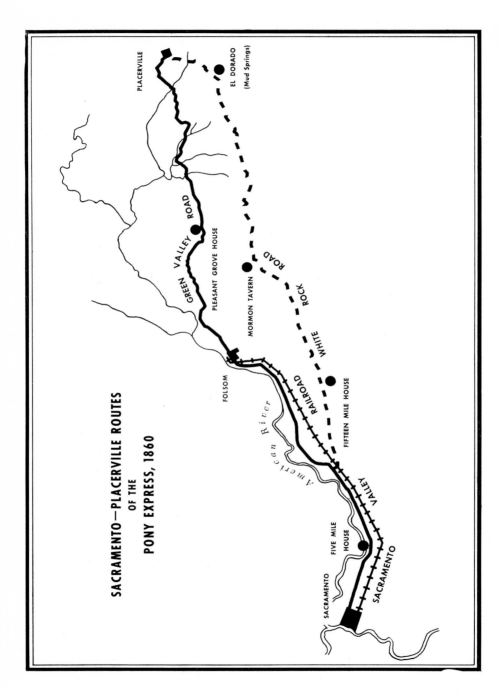

Comparison of Placerville-Sacramento Pony Express routes after mail was forwarded by railroad in July, 1860.

for the Pony Express Company. Your mails are . . . always ahead of time. I will do all in my power to forward your interests here." Further than that, this solid citizen of the frontier acted as postmaster, custodian of government funds, probate judge and justice of the peace.

The company was similarly fortunate in its appointment, by Superintendent A. E. Lewis, of an agent at Cottonwood Creek, two miles northeast of present-day Hanover, Kansas, the first station east of the notorious McCanles stop at Rock Creek. He was George H. Hollenberg, a native of Hannover, Germany, who after a series of youthful mining adventures in California, Australia and Peru, and in a shipwreck off the Florida coast, was advised by a doctor to go West.

About 1857, with his wife, Sophia, he enterprisingly selected a site on the Oregon trail that, with equal benefit, would serve as home, trading post and public hostelry. Hollenberg's substantial cabin, built on a slight rise of the ground, and his long stable nearby, attracted trade from overland emigrants, stage passengers, teamsters, and traveling military forces. The Hollenberg Station, as it is sometimes called, boasted a bar for thirsty travelers and provided an abundant table for its hungry guests. The owner deservedly prospered and hired clerks for his store, one of whom became postmaster at the station.

In 1874, at the age of 51, Hollenberg sailed for his former home in Germany, with the twofold purpose of vacationing and inducing emigration to his growing community. Four hours out of New York, aboard the steamer *Bolivia* bound for Glasgow, he suffered a hemorrhage of the lungs and died. He was buried at sea on July 1st.

West of Salt Lake City the nobility of man and the conveniences of his station rapidly deteriorated. This was the frontier in its most rugged complexion, where mere survival, utterly dependent upon supplies from Utah and California, was a paramount and continuing occupation. Nowhere was the staid dignity of the English traveler, Sir Richard Burton, so sorely tried by primordial living.

Dugway was abominable. Few men would have relished a station keeper's billet at this miserable, insignificant stop, 20 miles west of Egan's Station. It featured an architectural design no more complicated than a hole in the ground, four feet deep. The opening was roofed with split cedar through which, in an incongruous touch of civilization, poked an adobe chimney. Water was available only by the cask, hauled in by wagon.

Butte Station, 10 or 12 relays beyond, was by comparison, a commodious hotel. The cabin, a sandstone structure covered by a cedar roof, was about 30 feet long by 15 feet wide. The interior was handily divided into two rooms by a sheet of canvas hung between poles placed to support the roof. In one room two bedsteads, roughly constructed of wooden uprights stuck into the dirt floor, provided bunks for four men. Burton noted that the floor was a bit hilly, and that water, oozing in at the end of the cabin, left it wet.

In the other room his attention was attracted to a huge seven-foot fireplace, fitted with a long soup-pot hook. Along the walls protruding pegs supported such decorations as spurs, pistols, whips, gloves and leggings. The tables and benches were styled in rough-dressed lumber, while a more personal comfort was in disturbing primitiveness. "Soap," Burton complained, "was supplied by a handful of gravel, and evaporation was expected to act towel."

He observed that rifles and pistols hung all over the place, as did a goodly assortment of miscellaneous tools. For some reason left to the imagination, he noted this sturdy edifice was alternately and facetiously called Robbers' Roost and Thieves' Delight.

The knightly author's critical view of the crudities and discomforts of these frontier hostels temporarily turned into almost a compliment when, at Fort Churchill, on October 19, 1860, he was surprised to find that the military establishment "was tee-totalist and avoided cards like good Moslems." The fort was then in the process of construction and Captain Stewart, who had led California's Army contingent against the Pah-Utes, had planned the post buildings and was in charge of the forces stationed there. A rhomboid in shape, the reservation occupied 1,384 acres, adjoining Buckland's ranch on the banks of the Carson River, 20-odd miles east of Carson City.

Bolivar Roberts had made arrangements with Buckland to use his "good-sized cabin" as a Pony Express station, but apparently the rancher declined employment as keeper, for this position was taken by W. C. Marley. The place served as a rider-relay, or home station, until establishment of the fort, which became the easternmost terminal of Frederick Bee's telegraph line.

Samuel Sanford Buckland, like so many other early Nevadans, had been a gold-seeker in the California mines. He was born in Kirkersville, Licking County, Ohio, on September 13, 1826, and emigrated to California, via Panama, in 1850. After seven years' digging for precious glitter dirt, he joined James O. Williams (of Pah-Ute fame) in freighting supplies from Placerville to Genoa. This hardy enterprise was pursued by the packing of cargo on the backs of 10 mules, for which their patrons were assessed the reasonable rate of eight cents per pound.

This undertaking was of short duration, perhaps less than a year, and he was soon located on what was known as Nick Marlin's ranch. In post-Pony Express days he was a substantial agriculturist, owning 1,680 acres on which he resided in a commodious home, largely built with lumber salvaged from the abandoned Fort Churchill. His place was designated the County Seat of Churchill County.

Buckland died December 28, 1884, at the age of 58 and was buried in the iron-fenced family plot next to his wife, Eliza Ann, on a low knoll of Fort Churchill, overlooking his ranch. The gravesite was marked by an upright slab of white marble, which long since has toppled over, leaving a patchwork of pieces but a still legible inscription.

Sportsman Hall, on the western slope of the Sierras, was famous in Pony Express history as the home station where William Hamilton relinquished the first eastbound *mochila* to Warren Upson. It was one of the most colorful, crowded, and profitable establishments along the road to California. Snugly and solidly built among the towering pines and spruce of the vaulting mountains, it afforded two stories of food, hospitality and comfort for thousands of travelers threading their way over the precipitous wagon road between Placerville and Genoa.

Stagecoach "whips" and passengers, teamsters, mule drovers, horsemen, foot travelers, all found rest and relaxation inside its pine wood frame walls. Upwards of a hundred guests rode, walked or galloped of a night up to the Hall's wide pillared porch, seeking accommodation. A huge stable sheltered their horses, while an ample, smelly caldron of boiling lye in the yard at the rear gave olfactory assurance that there would be sufficient soap to wash away the dust and grime of travel.

John Blair, a cooper from Paisley, Scotland, built Sportsman Hall on a relatively level piece of mountain land, about 12 road miles east (and up) from Placerville. With his brother, James, he first had settled for a time in the east, where they were able to save enough money for John to buy into a wagon train destined for California. When James followed some time later, he found John running the Hall, having already done well in the lumber business. James then took over the management and reportedly operated the hostelry for 21 years. Twice it was struck by fire and each time rebuilt, finally being dismantled. Today a smaller, more modest stopping place of the same name serves motorized travelers only a few feet from the foundation of John Blair's original building.

Chapter Ten

DISTRESS AND INFAMY

Russell's arithmetic failed to add up even before he sent his son, John, the momentous telegram establishing the Pony Express. The shocking truth was that Russell, Majors & Waddell were close to, if not at, bankruptcy a full month before he determined to plunge into the venture—a fact of which Russell's partners were forlornly aware but which the proud financier himself, buoyant, optimistic and always manipulating, refused to recognize, much less admit. On and on he spun, riding the gay merry-go-round of hope, snatching up more bank loans on paper of doubtful virtue, fostering thoughts of new and bigger government contracts, and launching enterprises where the only certainty was the financial risk.

Theoretically, the combined assets of the partners exceeded liabilities by about $419,000. But unreported was a catastrophic loss of $150,000 in a herd of freight oxen, caught in a howling blizzard at Ruby Valley, Nevada. It had been decided to speculate the cattle on the California market, rather than return them to Leavenworth from Camp Floyd, Utah, to which they had pulled wagons of Army supplies. The loss reduced their margin of assets to $269,000—and their obligations due in December totaled $250,000. Someone had computed that, through the following June, notes and bills payable would breach the staggering sum of $1,000,000.

As though to keep from being discouraged, Russell busied himself organizing and selling stock in the Central Overland California & Pikes Peak Express Co., inaugurating the Pony, and bidding on the 1860-61 freighting contract. Late in 1859 he was certain the partnership would again haul the lion's share of military supplies, and hopefully looked forward to furnishing several thousand head of beef cattle for the Army in Utah, which by now was being reduced in strength. Moreover, he figured that Congress would be granting the partner's claim for $494,000 in losses suffered in 1857 on the way to Fort Bridger, when attacking Mormons destroyed several trains. And Congress, too, early this year, 1860, assuredly would quit its interminable bickering and finally provide the juiciest plum of all —a tri-weekly mail service over the Central Route.

On the twelfth of April the first of these hope-balloons suffered a slight deflation. Russell, Majors & Waddell signed a contract with the quartermaster at Fort Leavenworth—not for military supplies to Utah, which were to be hauled by others, but for freight to New Mexico only. Thus ended the monopoly on military hauling.

But the contract was substantial and the usual preparations were made. At Kansas City 1,500 wagons were shipped in and parked, great herds of cattle and mules were assembled, and two large warehouses were built to receive goods for outfitting the trains. Then, quietly, another catastrophe settled over the partners. Week after week, through May and June, normal departure months, they waited for orders to load and leave. There were men to pay, cattle to feed and, as usual, loans falling due. Not until August and September was there any appreciable tonnage to move, delaying the first earnings until fall.

Evidence of hard times cropped up all over the company, most frequently in repeated failures to meet the payroll. Somewhere along the route one wag converted Central Overland California & Pikes Peak Express into Clean Out of Cash and Poor Pay. Another penned a poetic threat which appeared on station walls:

> On or about the first of May,
> The boys would like to have their pay.
> If not paid by that day,
> The stock along the road may stray.

Out in Ruby Valley, William H. Shearman, an associate of Major Egan, began to hear grumbles from unpaid riders and other employees, and a number of them presented him with "certificates" attesting that they had been without pay for several months. Meanwhile, at Salt Lake City, Livingston, Bell & Co., suppliers to the Pony Express, were getting nervous over bills owing them, and before the end of next February would obtain a court order to attach all the company's stage and express horses "in this territory."

Russell hastened to New York to try to find some way to alleviate the crisis, arriving early in July. His hope for a mail contract this year over the Central Route was dashed; again Congress had backwashed. He was faced with the new costs of the Pony Express, plus the losses in the Nevada Indian raids. The outlook was dim, already the company owed money to everyone in sight and there was ominous talk of insolvency.

Disappointingly, New York yielded no help and, on July 11th, he boarded the train for Washington. With him was Luke Lea, a banker returning to his capital office of Suter, Lea & Co., in which Russell had a roundabout interest. Luther R. Smoot, his partner in Smoot, Russell & Co., a Leavenworth banking house, was also a member of Suter, Lea & Co., and when forming the Kansas firm had gratuitously included Lea as one of the founders. Lea purportedly was surprised but didn't bother to renounce the use of his name, even when he might have politely suggested it through Majors who visited his office three years afterward in the Spring of 1858. In effect, then, if not in fact, Lea and Russell were partners—a relationship that was to have sinister connotations six months hence.

As such, they were familiar with one another's business affairs and rather naturally fell to discussing the money problems that were inundating Russell, Majors & Waddell. While seated in the jouncing rail car, Russell sought Lea's advice on the availability in Washington of stocks and bonds which could be borrowed for 60 to 90 days and hypothecated, to bolster the company's sagging financial condition. Lea professed to know of no such sources and affirmed that the current money market was tight. But, Russell asked, didn't he know of a man whose name was something like "Baylor," about whom he had heard in New York? No, he didn't; he was, however, familiar with a man named Godard Bailey, who had recently sold some securities for a senator.

Bailey was a clerk in the office of the Commissioner of Indian Affairs, a bureau which Lea himself once headed in President Taylor's administration. The banker protested that he was not a prospect, that "he had no stocks or money, and was as poor as anybody." Lea would know, for he and Bailey were well acquainted in business matters, the clerk having, on occasion, facilitated the handling of his bank's commercial dealings in the bureau. From the ensuing discussion Russell learned that Bailey was, in a circuitous way, related to Secretary of War Floyd, his wife being the daughter of Floyd's cousin. That intelligence would have been of keen interest to him. Since 1858, Floyd had given him acceptances against future income on transportation contracts, and there were nearly $200,000 of these going to protest by the end of July, unless, somehow, money was raised to honor them.

This peculiar form of financing was a signal accomplishment for the smooth promoter, having obtained Floyd's agreement to issue them over the opposition of the Quartermaster General whose subordinate in Leavenworth issued the military haulage contracts. More noteworthy still, it was a private arrangement for the benefit of Russell, Majors & Waddell, and no other contractor enjoyed the privilege. Typically, the form of the acceptances was:

Washington City, September 13, 1860

$15,000

Eight months after date pay to our own order, at the Bank of the Republic, New York City, fifteen thousand dollars, for value received, and charge to account of our transportation contract of the 12th day of April, 1860.

RUSSELL, MAJORS & WADDELL

Hon. J. B. Floyd
Secretary of War

War Department, September 18, 1860

Accepted.

John B. Floyd
Secretary of War

The accommodating Secretary, in 1858, agreed not only to issue acceptances, but obligingly wrote to various banks, urging their purchase or discount, to quiet any doubts on the validity of this novel type of negotiable paper. Later, he admitted that every acceptance he gave ran against unearned money, so as to give Russell, Majors & Waddell "the credit of their contract." One letter from the War Department to an inquiring correspondent explained that, on due date, the acceptances could be presented to the Department for collection, but that, in actual practice, this was unnecessary, as Russell, Majors & Waddell had retired the paper. The implication is obvious: Russell raised money on the acceptances and also collected the contract earnings against which the acceptances were guaranteed! Early in 1861, out of a total of nearly $7,000,000 of acceptances written, an embarrassed, confused staff member of the War Department estimated that "a minimum" of $1,445,000 of the paper was still outstanding.

As the train approached Washington, Russell's problem seemed overwhelming. If the $200,000 in acceptances that he couldn't retire went to protest, Secretary Floyd—and Russell, Majors & Waddell—would be ruined. Furthermore, the need was not momentary; there was, then, between $800,000 and $1,000,000 owing on others not yet due. The whole business had been wrong from the start. Floyd had been warned by no less a person than President Buchanan: the acceptances simply were illegal.

Godard Bailey, therefore, was a drifting log to a drowning man. Russell had to grasp at anything, even a poor prospect like an obscure government clerk. Despite Lea's repeated protestations that Bailey could do nothing, Russell pressed him to see the man and advise him of the impending danger to Floyd.

At this juncture one may question why it was so important that Bailey be told. Did Russell believe the clerk would somehow convey a message to Floyd that he, Russell, couldn't? Or did Russell secretly have foreknowledge of tangible help from him? Unfortunately, the record is silent.

The following day, as promised, Lea went to Bailey's office and explained Russell's predicament, stating that Secretary Floyd would be forced to resign if the acceptances were allowed to go to protest. Bailey immediately went over to the War Department to get verification from Floyd himself, but found him closeted with an Army general. Instead, he talked with William R. Drinkard, the department's chief clerk, reportedly a close friend of the Secretary, who kept a memo record of the acceptances that were issued. Drinkard confirmed Lea's interpretation of the situation, and offered to introduce Bailey to Russell, who happened to be in the building at the time. That was done.

Left to themselves, Bailey disclosed to Russell that he had some state securities which he could loan and which could be hypothecated, provided the identical bonds were returned. To this Russell readily agreed, and later that same day, in the privacy of his rooming house, received from Bailey $150,000 worth of Missouri 6s and Tennessee 6s for which he gave a note on Russell, Majors & Waddell in like amount.

Before the day was out, the great man, his depressing crisis temporarily relieved, took the train to New York. With the assistance of Jerome B. Simpson, agent for the company, he disposed of the bonds on the best terms possible—less than two-thirds their redemption values—and then made a trip to Leavenworth, Kansas.

Inside of a month he was back, and obliged to face the demand of the bond holders for greater margin, due to a deteriorating market in state obligations. Meantime, his own financial condition had worsened, and he found it impossible to make up the difference. So again he went to Washington and asked Bailey to see him. Frankly, he recounted the present state of his dire circumstances. Some of the bonds were going to be sold by his lenders, the partners were still in an embarrassed financial condition, and there were more acceptances about to go to protest. Was there anything further Bailey could do?

The disclosure rocked the poor clerk back on his heels. Then, in turn, he shocked Russell with a confession. For the first time, according to the latter, Bailey told him that the bonds were not his to loan, that they belonged to the Indian Trust Fund of the Interior Department where they were held for the benefit of various Indian tribes, and that he was merely the custodian charged with their safekeeping.

It was a climax. Bailey asserted that if the bonds were not returned, he would be ruined. And Russell, thoroughly frightened, was without the means to recover them. "In the stress of my difficulties," he later explained, "I was in no condition, and, as I have said before, I had no time to weigh the responsibility, on the one hand of wrecking our firm, discrediting the War Department, and permitting the hypothecated bonds to be sold beyond my reach, against that on the other hand of accepting more bonds with which to protect those that I had already used."

So, he determined on the second alternative. Bailey, the next day, handed over a new lot of bonds, $387,000 worth of Missouris, South Carolinas and Floridas. He exchanged Russell's previous note for $150,000 for another covering the new total of $537,000, and specified that all the bonds were to be returned before March 4th. The date was when Bailey's term of office expired.

Immediately Russell hastened again to the financial marts in New York where he hypothecated all but the Florida securities, which were deemed little more than worthless. Strident threats of secession in the South, and the inept fiscal policies of Secretary of the Treasury Howell Cobb, had so reduced the attractiveness of government issues that even a recent Federal offering had failed of subscription. He returned the Floridas to Bailey and received an equivalent value in North Carolinas.

It was now September, 1860. Before the end of the month it was evident that, contrary to promises he had made to Bailey, the proceeds from the second lot of bonds were inadequate to buy up the first group and pay off the maturing acceptances. In October he frantically scraped the bottom of the money barrel, writing $270,000 more in acceptances—against transportation to be performed next year!—borrowing additional sums through Samuel & Allen, the company's St. Louis agents, and, thankfully, collecting nearly $161,000 due from the War Department.

Alas, it was to no avail. Once more, toward the end of November, he journeyed to Washington and called upon his benefactor for renewed help. By now Bailey was so deeply implicated that a further effort apparently seemed of little consequence. This time, on the same good promises as before, he delivered $333,000 of Missouri and Tennessee bonds, but insisted that the grand total of $870,000 be backed up by a like amount of acceptances. Russell consented to the stipulation and deposited $735,000 of this doubtful paper with him; and later, to allow time to get Secretary Floyd's signature, wrote another —his last—for the $135,000 balance.

Only a few days had passed when, on December 1st, Godard Bailey realized how hopeless the situation had become, how impossible it was to disentangle himself from the sorry mess. He sat down, probably in the seclusion of his home, and addressed a letter to his boss, Secretary of the Interior Jacob Thompson, and described the entire transaction, attributing it to his desire to save Secretary Floyd's reputation. No selfish motive on his part was involved, he said.

Three weeks later, after a series of delays and misunderstandings by intermediaries as to its delivery, the message— together with all Russell's acceptances, which Bailey had carefully packaged—wound up at the White House.

The reaction was instantaneous. The President ordered an inventory to be taken of the remaining bonds in the safe at Bailey's office. On December 24th the House of Representatives authorized a full-blown investigation and named a Select Committee, headed by Representative Isaac N. Morris of Illinois. The Committee quickly organized itself, hired a stenographer and opened the hearing on December 27th. Over two-score witnesses were examined and cross-examined, and from the evidence adduced the Committee suspected "tortuous windings of vast and complicated interests, and extensive, though concealed ramifications." A clearer finding on such sinister doings, however, was frustrated by "artful and unwilling" witnesses and an epidemic of poor memories.

Luke Lea was one who suffered from mental lapses, and he made it quite plain that he was afraid of damage to his reputation and business. On one point, though, he stood pat. He did not, he said, suggest to Bailey the "abstraction" of bonds to help Russell. But C. G. Wagner, a relative of Bailey's, to whom the clerk's confession was first made, stated Bailey told him that Lea did, in fact, raise the idea.

On the same day that the House authorized the investigation, Russell was arrested in his New York office. He was returned to Washington and jailed. The court set his bond at a monumental $500,000. Local friends were able to raise only $300,000, prolonging his discomfiture a few days until the bond was reduced. Bailey got off easier, on bail of $5,000, but likewise had to remain behind bars until the sum was raised. There Luke Lea visited the clerk twice. He was charged with three counts of larceny, and Russell with three counts of receiving stolen bonds. Both were charged jointly with receiving stolen bonds and conspiring to defraud the Federal government.

Being criminally accused, neither could be compelled to testify before the Select Committee, a right which Bailey was happy to take. Russell assumed a different attitude and voluntarily appeared, stating that "I claim to be an honest man and would prefer to make out a statement of the whole transaction in writing and have it spread on your records." The request was granted and in four days he reappeared with the statement. The Committee proceeded to interrogate him at length, obtaining his frank admission of receiving and disposing of the bonds, but when asked if he had ever paid, or given a present to anyone in connection with his business at the War Department, he balked and asked to consult counsel. The next day his attorney conferred with Chairman Morris, advising that Russell had no desire to withhold information but that the question was outside the scope of the Committee's investigation, adding that his client would answer if the House of Representatives authorized the question to be asked.

On the following day Russell showed up again, handed over his statement, which he described as fully explanatory, and left. Subsequently, the Committee ridiculed it, saying it fell short of making a clean breast of the whole affair. On one point in particular—suspected bribery—it threw no light whatever.

Within a week Russell's case was called in the Criminal Court of the District of Columbia. There his attorney must have been no less enterprising than himself, for the lawyer boldly argued that the defendant should go free. It was a Machiavellian maneuver. He pleaded the Act of 1857, which exempted witnesses before Congressional committees from later prosecution on the matter about which they had testified.

What cleverness! First indicted as a criminal, he could, by law, have chosen not to testify before the Committee and thereby incriminate himself. But taking the opposite course and, with a great show of cooperation, freely answering its questions, he neatly established an immunity against prosecution, and probable conviction.

Stymied, the court asked the members of the Select Committee to appear and testify on precisely what matters Russell had been questioned. The request was refused, with the explanation that the members could not do so until their report had been filed. In evident sheepishness it was averred that the Committee had not heard of the Act of 1857 until three days after Russell had testified. As it turned out, none of the members ever did appear in court, and the indictment was quashed late in March.

That same month Bailey was arraigned, and pleaded not guilty. In September, 1862, the case was called to trial, but the bond-embezzling clerk failed to appear and his bail was forfeited. Seven years later it was again called and the United States Attorney entered a *nolle prosequi,* ending the case.

A month after the hearing on Russell's indictment, the Select Committee was authorized by the House of Representatives to query him on making payments or gifts to government employees. The chairman sent off a telegram to him in New York, requesting that he appear, and at the same time wired Floyd in Virginia that, if he became implicated—a possibility fully expected—he would be permitted to attend.

Floyd, who had since resigned as Secretary of War, ignored the message. When three days passed and Russell failed to show up, Morris dispatched a U.S. Marshal to bring him in—something easier said than done. Diligent search by the officer failed to turn him up, and the obvious conclusion was that he had gone into hiding. The question of bribery was not the subject of any indictment and, therefore, his appearance, if not voluntary, could be compelled. For reasons best known to himself Russell did not intend to come forth either way. Early in February the Committee ended the inquiry without putting the crucial question.

Meanwhile, without waiting for the outcome of the court cases or the investigation Secretary of the Interior Jacob Thompson frantically attempted to recover the government's loss. In large advertisements in the daily press he listed the number of the "feloniously abstracted" bonds, advising the various states to stop payment on them and warning all persons against buying or receiving them.

It was a waste of effort. The government had brought suit against Godard Bailey, the Bank of the Republic and sundry other defendants, seeking return of the bonds. Late in February the U.S. District Court for the Southern District of New York decided that the bonds were negotiable and that all parties who had received them in good faith, without notice of their abstraction, were *bona fide* holders.

From almost the date of his indictment, well-meaning apologists have strived to whitewash or minimize Russell's guilt in the shocking scandal, alleging entrapment at the hands of a scheming administration of southerners who had nearly wrecked the national economy, and who sought a convenient whipping boy to appease the public clamor. Supposedly, Russell was "induced" by Bailey, acting as Floyd's foil, to take the bonds, enabling the cabinet officer to recover his illegal acceptances put up as security. Because the record is annoyingly

Fort Laramie, Nebraska Territory, as it was seen a few months before the Pony's inaugural run. From original in Library of Congress.

Log buildings and tents of Fort Kearny, Nebraska Territory, as they appeared in the year prior to the start of the Pony Express. Copied from a rare photograph in the Library of Congress.

Transmitting the Butterfield agreement of 1861, which reduced Russell, Majors & Waddell to subcontractor status, Russell's feeling evidently was of great relief — for getting half a loaf instead of none. A transcript of his writing is given below.*

*W. B. Wadddell, Lexington, Mo.

   Sir

   I herewith enclose copies of the contracts I have made under the authority delegated to me by the Co. and believing them to be all the Co. could ask & as much as I ever encouraged them to hope for and with all an A No. 1 contract one that will pay them big money if well managed. I am very content. We should get the thing up all right, work it with energy and with its results relieve entirely R M W.

   I am detained preparing my public statement. Fear I cannot get off til last this week. Yrs

                                                                    W. H. Russell

Bancroft Library

Advert'sing the takeover of the Pony Express in the San Francisco *Evening Bulletin,* June 28, 1861. The Overland Mail Co., below, points out that departures are dependent on arrival of Pony mail from San Francisco, under the control of Wells, Fargo, as made clear in the ad at left. At San Francisco, Wells Fargo expects to profit a dime on every letter envelope, while at Placerville the regular 10¢ government issue suffices.

Bancroft Library

PONY EXPRESS!

CHANGE OF

TIME!

NEWS!!

REDUCED

RATES!

10 Days to San Francisco!

LETTERS

WILL BE RECEIVED AT THE

OFFICE, 84 BROADWAY,

NEW YORK,

Up to **4** P. M. every TUESDAY,

AND

Up to **2½** P. M. every SATURDAY,

Which will be forwarded to connect with the PONY EXPRESS leaving
ST. JOSEPH, Missouri,

Every WEDNESDAY and SATURDAY at 11 P. M.

TELEGRAMS

Sent to Fort Kearney on the mornings of MONDAY and FRIDAY, will connect with **PONY** leaving St. Joseph, WEDNESDAYS and SATURDAYS.

EXPRESS CHARGES.

LETTERS weighing half ounce or under **$1 00**
For every additional half ounce or fraction of an ounce 1 00
In all cases to be enclosed in 10 cent Government Stamped Envelopes,
And all Express CHARGES Pre-paid.

☞ PONY EXPRESS ENVELOPES For Sale at our Office.

WELLS, FARGO & CO., Ag'ts.

New York, July 1, 1861.

Wells Fargo's influence began to bear heavily on the Pony Express operation in the Spring of 1861,
culminating in a general assumption of agencies in the big eastern cities and the far West. In the
above ad, evidently a handbill, Wells Fargo appeals for business in New York under the reduced
rate of $1, effective July 1st.

quiet on whether Russell had foreknowledge of embezzling possibilities with Bailey, the obscure clerk is tacitly assigned a greater degree of guilt.

All of which has the whole essence of poppycock. The great promoter, founder of an empire in overland transport and tycoon of myriad enterprises across the breadth of the land, was, at the time, a mature, sophisticated man of 48, keen of intellect, and an able companion of famous men on the high-road of government, finance and industry. Friends were patently naive who could honestly credit such a man with blissful ignorance in manipulating those financial curiosities, the ubiquitous acceptances, or lightly overlook his responsibility in accepting a king's ransom in negotiable securities from an unknown clerk.

Plainly, the mess was of his own making. "Russell, Majors & Waddell not only absorbed all the sums earned by them under their contracts, and sold all the bonds they received from Mr. Bailey," the Select Committee disclosed, "but also raised very large sums of money upon the acceptances by the Secretary of War." Where, then, was the money to redeem the acceptances? At this point Russell's vaunted arithmetic was an exercise in futility.

If, through the artful practice of law, he was saved from the censure of legal guilt, there still remained the question of moral involvement. Abraham Lincoln answered that in correspondence with the Attorney General a week after his inauguration, when he alluded to the scandal, not as Bailey's perfidy, but as "the Russell fraud."

Chapter Eleven

THE DEMISE

██N THE SAME MONTH—December, 1860—that the bond scandal broke, the Thirty-Sixth Congress convened its second session and once again commenced the annual ruckus over the vexing question of the overland mail. It was the third attempt in as many years, since the Butterfield interests won the southern line, to gain recognition for the Central Route.

The credit of the Post Office Department was imperiled in 1859 by failure of the legislators to provide even the regular annual appropriation, much less authority for a duplicate mail service. In the next try during the spring of 1860 Russell nearly squeaked through with his gamble on the Pony Express. While applause for the equine mail was still ringing in the nation's press, not quite drowning out the threatening crescendo of Indian attacks, the Senate fought out and finally passed Senator Hale's bill. It provided for a daily service on the Central Route, weekly departures on a proposed northern line between St. Paul and The Dalles, Oregon, and a temporary ocean mail contract. But the bill reached the House in the last hour of June 25th, the final day of the session, and that body flatly refused to consider the measure on such brief notice.

Now once more the lines were sharply drawn, the southerners remaining as antagonistic as ever to any route through territory out of their control, the northerners holding fast for their scheme of full, through service and frequent deliveries to California over the shorter Central Route.

Despite all the sound and fury, however, the Post Route Bill enjoyed surprisingly good progress and early in February reached the upper house. In it was a provision for daily mail between California and the Missouri River for which the government would pay not over $800,000 per year.

Russell's optimism flew high. His inquisition by the Select Committee was ended, the inquiry having been closed February 8th, and he had already cleared the indictment hurdle. In a letter to Waddell he expressed "great faith in getting the mail contract, all right."

Hardly had the Senate begun deliberations when sobering advice reached the capital: Confederate forces had cut the Butterfield line near Fort Chadbourne, its stages had been stopped and the movement of mail halted. As it eventually turned out, the accused Texas Rangers actually hadn't stopped stages but merely had appropriated a large amount of the company's grain and several horses. The mail delay had taken place coincidentally, when Indians swooped down on the line in the treacherous Apache Pass.

But the first word, coming at the climax of national tension, gave Washington the jitters. The danger was all too apparent. Prominent voices in California had been loudly sympathetic with the southern cause. The Golden State's strategic location and Midas-like mineral wealth were rich prizes for both secessionists and loyalists—prizes the Union could ill afford to lose on default, for lack of an unbroken line of communication.

The Senate acted quickly. Less than a week after the foreboding news hit the capital, its Finance Committee reported out the annual Post Office Appropriation Bill. When it came up for vote on the floor, Senator Wilson tacked on an amendment, providing that the Butterfield line be transferred to the Central Route, the effect of which would eliminate bidding for the contract. William M. Gwin, a staunch friend of the Central Overland California & Pikes Peak Express, who was serving his last days as U.S. Senator, protested this arrangement, stating that it was unfair simply to shut out the men who had started the Pony Express, and who were then running a semimonthly stage over the Central Route.

His logical and persuasive argument almost resulted in an entirely different history of stagecoaching and mail service to the West. On February 28, 1861, Wilson's amendment carried on the Senate floor by the slim margin of only two votes, 21 to 19. Afterward, the House concurred in it more liberally, 117 to 43.

Butterfield's acceptance of the terms of the new law was required not later than March 25th, or its current contract would be cancelled and the Central Route thrown open to bid. Doing so, the line had to surrender all claims against the government arising out of prior operations over the Southern Route. The law specified that the daily letter mail would be delivered in 23 days' running time, while "heavy" mail, including newspapers, could be transported by ocean steamer at the option and expense of the contractor. Denver was to share in the new service, on a less frequent, tri-weekly schedule.

The Pony would be continued. "They [the contractors] shall also be required during the continuance of their contract, or until the completion of the overland telegraph, to run a pony express semiweekly at a schedule time of 10 days eight months and 12 days four months, carrying for the government free of charge, five pounds of mail matter, with the liberty of charging the public for transportation of letters by said express not exceeding one dollar per half ounce."

Pay for the entire service was set, by amendment to the bill, at $1,000,000 per year, with an additional $100,000, representing two months' postal revenue over the Southern Route, to be paid Butterfield for expenses and "damages" incurred in moving to the Central Route.

Russell's "great faith" in winning the coveted mail contract was obviously from a more modest viewpoint than as the reigning lord of the Central. A few days after Godard Bailey broke confidence and shattered his world of financial sophistry, he conceded to Waddell that a through mail line to the Pacific Coast was beyond the company's means—"the whole line will require too much additional capital and we have it not." Such a doleful admission of failure! So that flamboyant gesture, the great wager that sent scores of young lads racing across the prairies, had come to naught. What now was he thinking of the gloried Pony Express? How ironical that his pains to prove the Central Route feasible should benefit an arch rival!

Perhaps the thought was of no consequence, for the inimitable promoter was a man of doing, not apt to be deterred by introspection or spilled milk. Sometime between his admission that the bet was lost and the day that Senator Wilson proposed his amendment, Russell evidently went into a huddle with the Butterfield people and worked out arrangements for a joint operation of the upcoming contract. It wasn't exactly a secret that they had met; only the details were kept quiet. California's junior senator, Milton S. Latham, said the Overland Mail outfit was going to buy the Central Route line, an indication that he was as much in the dark as Gwin, who argued against the arbitrary gift of the contract, believing Russell financially able to swing it.

During the Senate's argument over the rate of pay—initially proposed by Wilson as $1,150,000 per year—Latham made it fairly clear that Russell had withdrawn as a contender. "The present contractors running that service," he said, referring to the Central Route, "have signified an unwillingness to carry this mail matter at the rate of $1,000,000. I refer to Mr. Russell, or the California and Pike's Peak Express Company, as it is usually denominated, of which he is the president. Therefore, I do not see that any injury can be done to them." In cahoots now with his onetime competitor, obviously Russell's sole purpose was to let Butterfield have the contract, which was too big a thing for a pathetic bankrupt to handle, and then share in the proceeds as a working partner. Thus, by calling it quits, he helped clear the legislative decks.

On invitation of the Postmaster General, Latham and Representative Schuyler Colfax aided in settling details of the new law with the Butterfield men, and they accepted the contract on March 12, 1861. Four days later, in New York, Russell and William B. Dinsmore, who became president of the Overland Mail Co. the previous April, affixed their signatures to a joint-operation agreement. It provided that the Central Overland California & Pikes Peak Express would give service from the Missouri River to Salt Lake City, connecting there with Overland Mail stages which would carry the mail and passengers over the balance of the route to California.

Russell's company was to receive $470,000 annually as its portion of the mail revenue, and receipts of the Pony Express were to be divided equally. Dinsmore's company was to take 30 percent of all revenue accruing from local express and passenger service over Russell's part of the line. A superintendent, appointed by the Overland Mail and paid by both firms, was to have over-all charge of the combined service.

On the same day Russell signed another contract to clear out competition and give the new syndicate an unmolested monopoly on express and passenger traffic beyond the Missouri River. E. S. Alford, president of the Western Stage Company, agreed to pull his stages off the route between Fort Kearny and Denver, but to continue running a feeder line between Omaha and the Fort, to connect with the new operation. The curtailment was worth $20,000 a year to Alford, $14,000 to be paid by Russell's firm which would haul the required tri-weekly Denver mail, and $6,000 by the Overland company.

In a way, the famed entrepreneur's dream for a big mail contract had come true. To be sure, it was only as a subcontractor that the company's stages would now roll westward, traversing just a portion of the route. But it still was the biggest contract the stage line had ever held. Russell was reconciled to it. The circumstances were vastly changed from the salad days of a year before, when he set the Pony a-flying and received the admiring accolade of a grateful country. To Waddell he wrote that the arrangements were "all the company could ask for . . . and with all an A No. 1 contract I am content."

Soon he was out West again, and on April 26th attended a meeting of the board of directors. On what appears to have been an earlier understanding, he offered his resignation as president and it was accepted. He retained his seat on the board, while Bela M. Hughes, an eminent lawyer, was elected to the head post.

Shortly the Overland Mail Co. was reported busily engaged in making plans to occupy the route west of Salt Lake City. The mileage it would be responsible for was only about a fifth of what its coaches had traveled on the Southern Route where it had maintained 160-odd stations, and the switch resulted in a surplus of stock and equipment. The greater part of this was disposed of to the Central Overland California & Pikes Peak Express.

On June 5th the Overland Mail management called a meeting at Salt Lake City to work out details of inaugurating the daily mail on July 1st. James E. Bromley, division superintendent for Russell east of Salt Lake City, Major Howard Egan and Bolivar Roberts represented the Central Overland. The conferees tentatively agreed on plans for the Overland Mail Co. to place some 600 horses along the road as far as Virginia City, together with 25 stagecoaches, 25 drivers and 12 conductors, plus station keepers and stock tenders, a total of nearly 150 men. Part of the stock and carriages arrived on June 24th, when E. R. Purple, a Butterfield employee, reported in at Fort

Crittenden (the new name of Camp Floyd) from Yuma with 120 head of horses and 10 Concord wagons.

On July 1st the changeover was official. The country's first daily overland stage service commenced from either end of the long route to the west. And the Pony Express, for the first time, became a subsidized postal operation. There was little public ado, for, after all, this ultimate development in overland transport had been evolving for a dozen years, ever since James Marshall had plucked a few yellow pebbles from the race of Sutter's mill. Disappointingly, that great champion of adequate mail service, the *Alta California,* gave only passing notice to the arrival at San Francisco on July 18th of the first daily stage from St. Louis.

Meanwhile, Russell's step-down had relieved him of executive status and the responsibility of inventing new tricks in financial wizardry to keep the ponies running and the stages rolling. Generously, though, he was willing to lend what talents he could during the period of management transition—an offer that neither Majors nor Waddell could make, for both, by now, were out of the picture.

Since the bond debacle in Washington, all three of the partners had busied themselves totaling up assets and liabilities, and penning numerous deeds of trust to quiet clamouring creditors, who had been deprived even of the uncertain hope in the notorious acceptances. Majors, washed out completely, pathetically returned to his old, initial role as a small-time private freighter. Waddell simply retired to the serenity of his home, which he ingeniously retained for his comfort by deeding it to his son.

Only Russell remained on the scene, mainly because some of his property had become so entwined with that of the firm that it could not readily be disposed of. En route to the board of directors meeting and his pending resignation, he had stopped at St. Louis and conferred with General Superin-

Bela M. Hughes, the lawyer-turned-expressman who succeeded Russell as president of the Central Overland California & Pikes Peak Express.

Benjamin Holladay, heavy creditor to the Pony Express and stagecoach operations. Through foreclosure he became the proprietor of the Central Overland California & Pikes Peak Express Co.

John Butterfield, guiding light of the Butterfield Overland Mail Company until he was "deposed" in the spring of 1860.

Harry L. Roff, often named as the first Pony Express rider out of Sacramento. Photo taken about 1913.

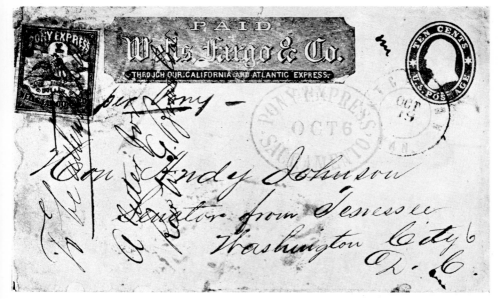

Envelope addressed to Senator Andrew Johnson bears a Wells Fargo $1 (red) running horse stamp, issued after July 1, 1861. Hand cancellations show it was mailed at Marysville, Calif. (impression, upper left, not reproducible), received at Sacramento October 6th, and arrived at Atchison, at that time the terminus of the Pony, on October 19th.

The small, $1 double-circle stamp, evidencing payment for weight in excess of the first half-ounce, makes this envelope a collector's item. Only three such covers are known to exist. Envelopes with this intricate WF&C design came into use after the Pony became subsidized with the 1861 mail contract.

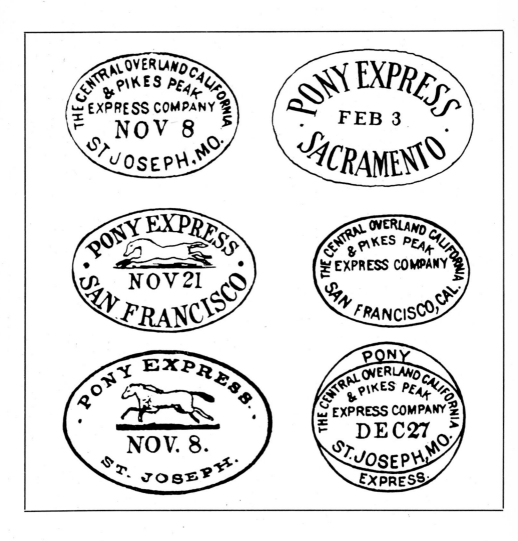

Hand franks used at Pony Express offices to evidence payment of charges for the courier service. Envelopes generally were stamped with two such devices, one marking receipt at the Pony office of origin, and the second one arrival at the destination office. In addition to these designs, occasionally there is found a PAID stamp in an oval shape, sometimes incorporating the words, "California Pony Express." After the advent of Wells, Fargo & Co., new franks were apparently devised, eliminating the running horse in the San Francisco and St. Joseph impressions.

tendent Alvord of the Butterfield line, to work out details of the
new contract's operation. Alvord accompanied him to St. Joseph
and thence to Leavenworth. After the meeting, with Hughes in
tow, they stagecoached to Denver to select a new route for the
daily mail via the booming Pikes Peak area, but its use was
delayed until some eight months after the Pony's finale.

Undaunted by the crushing blows of the last six months to
his reputation, credit and honor, the effervescent promoter gave
Colorado a stunning demonstration of his recuperative powers.
In an amazing encore of freewheeling initiative, he took hold
of several parcels of promising real estate, organized a couple
of wagon road companies in anticipation of profits from the
Pacific railroad, and hopefully developed gold mining ventures.

New York, however, was more abundantly populated with
speculators of means, and, leaving his family in Missouri, he
moved there in 1865 to open a brokerage office specializing in
mining stocks. Continuing to borrow money from old friends,
but in reduced amounts, and living in a second-rate rooming
house, this futile skirmish against the ramparts of finance
proved to be the pitiful last act for the once-grand impresario
of money magic. Within a few months he was again resorting to
deeds of trust to cover liabilities, and in the next year was list-
ing a debt for groceries. Where a proud man had walked with
the mighty and spoke with influence, he now moved in musty
obscurity. With declining health and fortunes there was barely
time for a last curtain call—as a patent medicine salesman.

Bela M. Hughes may have been a good lawyer; he was no
businessman, surely not the equal of Russell. When he climbed
into the saddle of the Central California Overland & Pikes
Peak Express, he found himself astride a moribund horse and,
whether by choice or circumstance, he was to ride the battered
carcass to the bitter end. Russell's staggering legacy of unpaid
bills, bank obligations and promissory notes was about to prove
too great a burden for this conventional man—or his dying horse
—to carry alone.

Scarcely had the new president donned his spurs when he was obliged to apply for relief and succor to Ben Holladay, who already had established himself as a creditor of the Pony in another era. Preparations for the new daily service were monumental, calling for more men, equipment, supplies, stages and horses all along the line. Money was in critical need, and Holladay supplied it generously. On July 1st, when the new government contract took effect, he was able to total up $200,000 which he had advanced on drafts.

This former frontier rustic, dram shop proprietor, scout, trader, merchant and partner of the great Russell was a fast-rising light in the country's expanding commerce. Few were his equal for sheer audacity and unmitigated nerve. Surely he was not blind to the precarious credit of the debtor company which, he said, already owed him $500,000 on previous advances for wages, feed and provisions. Surely he was not blind to opportunity.

Futilely, Hughes tried to stave him off. On July 5, 1861, he called a board meeting to approve issuance to Holladay of a note and deed of trust on the company. Through some delay, this wasn't accomplished until the following November, when he was given a bond of $400,000 and a three-year mortgage. The maneuver was hopeless. Inside of a month, the impatient Holladay declared the bond forfeit and moved for foreclosure. At a public sale early the following March he bid the company in at $100,000 and became the new owner.

Meanwhile, oblivious to all the financial jockeying back in Missouri, the Pony Express continued to run with greater popularity than ever, its patrons increased by the reduction in rate, on July 1st, to $1 per half ounce, from the $2 charge set the previous April. Current Pony deliveries at San Francisco were running at the rate of 91 letters, as against 64 during the preceding three months. California letter writers were still the best customers, sending three missives eastward for every one brought west.

Sharing in the increase was a multiplicity of carriers, for the handling of mail in California had undergone a change with the advent of the Overland Mail beyond Salt Lake. From Carson City, via Virginia City, to Placerville, the company had sublet its daily stint in stagecoaches to the Pioneer Line, under the flourishing proprietorship of Louis McLane, and retained for itself only the Salt Lake-Carson City segment of the route.

West of Carson City, Wells, Fargo & Co. stepped in to fill the gap in Pony service, functioning as agent of the Overland Mail Co. to Placerville, the end of the route under the new law. Californians, and particularly the daily press, were upset by the government's cutoff here of the speedy letter delivery and urgently suggested extension of the Pony by private enterprise. This was done by Wells, Fargo simply by retaining the existing service into San Francisco and operating it under its own auspices. Commencing July 1, 1861, the route and service, then, remained identical to that previously offered by the Pony's initial operators.

Only the charges varied. Wells, Fargo engaged Britton & Rey, San Francisco lithographers, to print new adhesive stamps in a running horse design to evidence prepayment of the new $1 per half-ounce fee. Denominations were $1 in a red stamp, $2 in a green and $4 in a black, each measuring 21 x 24¼ mm. The same stamps were applied whether the Pony Express accepted a letter at San Francisco, Sacramento or Placerville, or even at off-line agencies at various points in California, and were good for through service to St. Joseph. In accordance with postal regulations, patrons had to enclose their letters in 10-cent government-stamped envelopes, which the company supplied at San Francisco, printed with its own frank, at 20 cents each. Private, or ordinary, envelopes incurred a penalty of 25 cents. (At Placerville, however, covers sold for only 10 cents, so as not to exceed the authorized Pony rate of $1, effective eastward of that point.) Although the original idea was that the new-issue stamps would be supplied at both ends of the route, they were used only on envelopes mailed from the West.

Conversely, a small round stamp, made available at the same time, was occasionally used exclusively in the East on westbound mail, supposedly to cover fees in excess of the first half-ounce rate. This frank, deep blue in color, had a $1 value and was printed in the "garter," or double-circle, design and measured 15½ mm in diameter.

All of these were Wells, Fargo's second venture in the printing of express stamps. Something akin to a general take-over by the express firm of the entire Pony management appears to have occurred in the spring of 1861, following Butterfield's winning of the big contract. On April 1st the company became agents of the Pony at San Francisco, instead of the Alta Tele-graph Co., and the rate for letters was dropped to $2 per half-ounce. At this time Britton & Rey were assigned to do the first adhesive stamps ever used on Pony letters, a $2 red and a $4 green of the design already described.

It was hardly an expense that would have been assumed by a single isolated agency—which clearly they were not. By May 16th, at Russell's order, Wells, Fargo had taken up the agency at Sacramento. Previously, they had moved into the agency setup in the East, becoming the Pony Express repre-sentative at St. Louis, but designated the U.S. Express to act for them there. Similar arrangements followed at other major metropolitan cities—including New York, Boston, Philadelphia and Chicago—the U.S. Express and the American Express act-ing under the auspices of Wells, Fargo "so that the number of agents throughout the country has been doubled," according to a contemporary report.

Substantial evidence suggests that Wells, Fargo & Co.'s participation at this time in the movement of mail overland may have been of greater proportion than merely as carriers of the Pony mail. Early in April, 1860, New York and San Francisco papers reported that the firm had acquired control of the Butterfield Overland Mail Co. It was the same month that John Butterfield was replaced by Dinsmore.

Even before then it was plain that the financial fabric of the Butterfield company was largely woven with skeins of Wells, Fargo yarn. From the early 1850's Henry Wells and William G. Fargo had participated in a lion's share of the eastern states' express business through interlocking directorates in principal firms. Out of 11 signatures on the September 16, 1857, contract with the Government, which originally put Butterfield into business on the Southern Route, no less than five —including Fargo himself—were of Wells, Fargo associates.

It is of little wonder, then, that the contract signed by Russell and Dinsmore reserved to Wells, Fargo the exclusive right to express business moving east and west on the combined lines through Salt Lake City. In 1861 the lusty company boosted its capital stock to $1,000,000, following a previous increase in 1860, and had established itself as a major contender for the country's express cargo by swallowing up smaller firms as rapidly as it could. As the dominant owner of the Butterfield line, its relationship to the overland mail operations west of Salt Lake City, therefore, would have been identical to that of Russell, Majors & Waddell, onetime principal stockholders of the Central Overland California & Pikes Peak Express.

From the time that the Pony Express became "official" with a government subsidy, its days were numbered. The singing wire of the telegraph, in less than four months, would forever end its usefulness. Congress, failing in 1860 to give Russell his mail contract, did better by the electrical telegraph, agreeing to underwrite a concession for a line from the Missouri River to California. As first drawn, the bill was an outright gift to Hiram Sibley, but as finally passed, it ordered the Secretary of the Treasury to advertise for bids on construction of a telegraph system inside of two years, beginning July 31, 1860. Preferential use was reserved to the government for 10 years, and the rate of $3 for 10 words, from the Missouri River to San Francisco, was authorized. The contractor was given the right to cut trees from public land for poles. As already related, through the curious circumstance of three lower bidders withdrawing, Sibley, the highest bidder, was awarded the contract at a guaranteed government use of $40,000 per year.

No route for the wire was specified in the act, though Sibley had long stumped for a line of poles along the Central Route. Edward Creighton, a successful line constructor, had examined the Southern Route, via Fort Smith, in 1859. Then, early in 1860, astride a mule, he traveled the Central from Omaha to Sacramento, and announced his willingness to build on that route.

Western Union, as such, was not behind Sibley, for the company did not wish to risk its sinews and prestige on such a hazardous venture. So he enlisted the help of less conservative individuals, among whom were Jeptha H. Wade of the Erie & Michigan Telegraph, Dr. Norvin Green, Southwestern Telegraph Co., and Charles M. Stebbins, Missouri & Western Telegraph Co. These men, along with Frederick A. Bee, Benjamin F. Ficklin and Edward Creighton, were included in the roster of incorporators of the Pacific Telegraph Co., chartered by the Territory of Nebraska on June 11, 1861. Wade was elected president.

To gain additional working capital, the telegraph companies in California were offered a clever idea. If they would consolidate to build the western end of the line to Salt Lake City, they could share in the profits. Wade, later described as a "pious-looking party with a Methodist preacher's shaven upper lip and beard . . . who could horse-trade an opponent plumb out of his eyeteeth," went to California with A. W. Bee, to bring this about, and did so.

The new California syndicate adopted the name of the Overland Telegraph Company, and commenced to rebuild Bee's dilapidated old line between Placerville and Fort Churchill late in May, 1861. Sibley's group didn't break ground until July 4th at Fort Kearny. A wire had been extended that far from Omaha the previous autumn, in the gamble that the full line would be organized. Since then, the Pony Express had been stopping at Fort Kearny to pick up messages for California.

It had been agreed that the first company to string a line into Salt Lake City would take all the revenue over the full route until the wire was tied together, and that the losing company would pay the winner $50 a day until that was accomplished. Thus began one of the wildest construction races in the annals of American history. At both ends of the line crews worked at a feverish pitch. Independent contractors found plenty of work, cutting poles, hauling supplies and furnishing transportation. Even Brigham Young shared in this brief business boom. Creighton led the crews of the Pacific Telegraph Co., and James Gamble had charge of construction for the Overland Telegraph Co. Each of the two forces divided itself, working from both ends toward the middle. Poles were set at the rate of about five miles a day, and Pony riders, stopping for messages to add to their letter mail, found the advancing telegraph stations rapidly shrinking the distance between east and west.

The speed of construction entailed frequent confusion for the Pony Express, the arrival of a rider often failing to coincide with receipt of dispatches at the furthermost station. Sometimes the breakdown of service was unavoidable, as explained in this dispatch, published in the San Francisco *Bulletin*, August 17:

> Outer Station, Pacific Telegraph, 50 miles west of Kearny, August 9. Owing to moving the outer station from Kearny to this place on Tuesday and Wednesday, and line being down yesterday and today, I have not been able to get a word of news for this Pony.

The interruptions were understandable and no one was greatly concerned, for the long-sought telegraph was soon to be a reality. Sweating teams of pole setters kept pushing forward as fast as the supply of freshly cut trees permitted, and were regularly advised of progress being made at the opposite end as each Pony rider sped by.

Late in October another message delay occurred, this time of more significance. The *Alta* complained on the 22nd that "the Pony Express arrived at Ruby Valley the previous evening, but did not bring any dispatches. The operator at the end of the line could give no explanation." What the paper didn't know was that the race was over. Creighton's crew had won on October 18th, when the Pacific Telegraph Co. opened its line from Salt Lake City to Omaha.

First to flow over it was a rash of congratulatory messages, among them a felicitation from Brigham Young to President Jeptha Wade of the telegraph company, and an exchange of greetings between Acting Governor Fuller of Utah and President Lincoln. Six days later, on October 24th, James Gamble had his western end of the line hooked in, and the gap was bridged.

A flood of commercial dispatches crowded hard on the wire, as businessmen at both ends of the continent eagerly tried the wonderful new toy. Immediately there was a temporary jam-up of facilities, and tempers flared over annoying delays. One message that managed to slip through the melee of clicking keys, seemingly with urgent handling, was addressed to Wells, Fargo & Co. in San Francisco. The Pony Express, it instructed, would be halted forthwith. Thereupon the company, on October 25th, prepared a small advertisement for the press, advising the public that the equine mail was no more.

Thus was the hasty, thankless dismissal of a faithful friend. Here today, useful, even indispensable, the glory-decked steed and his noble rider were summarily discarded for the morrow, paid off as it were with a few cold, impersonal lines of black type. Nostalgically, the editor of the Sacramento *Bee* rushed to observe that it was no disgrace for the wilderness-overcoming, swift-footed messenger to have been encompassed, overthrown and routed by "a senseless, soulless thing that eats not, sleeps not and tires not, and knows not the difference between a rod of ground and the circumference of the globe."

But it was not the end—yet. For, like water in a pipe, the long communication line had to be drained of its flow of missives. While newspaper readers were sighing over loss of the valiant Pony, a lone rider spurred his horse across the wasteland somewhere beyond Salt Lake City, hurrying westward with a bulging *mochila*, containing 153 letters for San Francisco alone. Four days behind him was one more rider who left Atchison, Kansas, October 25th, the day of the advertisement. He was to be the last of the famous couriers, and his arrival in California in the first few days of November would write finis to a glorious episode.

Then, quite unexpectedly, after the last tear of leave-taking had been wiped away, like a phantom ghost another Pony appeared on November 21st, bringing a *mochila* of 103 letters. Was this, finally, the end? Who knows for sure? The shuttling, ethereal Pegasus, as late as December 4th, was still being credited for dispatches in the news columns of a loyal, steadfast patron, the *Alta*. But whenever his final ride, whenever the last farewell, the Pony's demise was at hand. Eclipsed by the march of science, his work was done.

His work—that's an interesting point. It may be well to cast the account, to see just what he did do.

First, consider his speculating founder. For the optimistic, hopeful Russell he accomplished precisely nothing, except to help push him deeper into the mire of debt and, hence, disrepute, remitting to him only a timeless fame and memory.

As for the telegraph, it's been said that the brass key followed in the Pony's train, as he virtually pulled the wire ends together. Truthfully, the honor is not his; the staccato messages would have come anyway. Congress, having long listened to the importunities of the telegraph advocates, finally approved the stringing of wire even before the horse express had proved it could pierce the wintry blast of snow over the Central Route. Sibley went on to win the issue while this fable of impassability was still a Southerner's argument.

Well, surely the Pony must be given credit as the forerunner of the Pacific Railroad, so profoundly forecast when Mayor Jeff Thompson slapped the hindquarter of the first impatient steed at St. Joseph. Didn't the gaily attired post rider, together with his fellow expressmen, beat a path approximately followed by the legions of track layers? Happily, that is true, but actually, the belching giant of steam and smoke was wooed by western expansionists long before the equine mail was even a dream, and its wheels were set a-rolling not by the pretentious Pony but by talented promoters and an all-Northern Congress. No, Russell's brief hope was only the predecessor, not the pathfinder, and neither the cause nor procurer, of the iron horse.

What, then, *did* the fame-ridden charger do? Plainly, he carried the mail. That was his means to the end, and the end was Russell's gamble.

Exactly what was the monetary worth of the Pony as a stake in this fabulous wager has been debated for years. At the outset, merely to equip the stations along the road with stock and provisions cost $70,000, according to an observation by Ben Holladay at the time. His conjecture on monthly expenses was that they would "foot up to $4,000, at least." Long afterward, Alexander Majors simply dismissed the experiment as a loss of several hundred thousand dollars. In the spring of 1861, Russell said that, during four months of the preceding winter, the eastbound mail between San Francisco and Roberts Creek was run at a loss of over $10,000. At Sacramento, one of his contemporaries who had a mind for figures, calculated that depreciation on investment and operating expenses put the monthly cost at $52,200. An eastern newspaper set the cost at "only $500" for each trip. Scribes of later times have strived to find the elusive answer by subtracting an estimated half-million dollars in receipts from an arbitrary $700,000 in expenses.

Whatever the pecuniary loss, in retrospect the Pony's very failure appears to have worked like a bright polish on the radiant sheen of his splendor. Poverty seems to have beautified and strengthened his indomitable spirit and courage and encompassed his memory in a misty aura of legend and fantasy. In passing he bequeathed a remarkable tale of proudly carried tradition, stirring romance and youthful bravery that lives forever.

Onward, onward, he rushed, dutifully bringing the tidings, glad or sad. Fearlessly, his rider explored the unknown desert, crossed the raging streams and swept through the pathless forest. He shined on mountain tops and raced with the wind through narrow valleys. Day and night, in rain or sleet, under blue skies or in blinding snow, his footsteps never paused, save in the pitiless agony of savage death. He bridged a vast gulf and made a continent, and he thrilled a waiting people with news of faraway places. He kept the vigil of needed trust. And in each generation the imperishable legend is born anew, as muffled hoofbeats once more echo the romantic story of the Old West.

BIBLIOGRAPHY

Alter, Cecil J., *Utah, The Storied Domain,* Vol. I, Chicago and New York, 1932.

Bailey, W. F., *The Pony Express,* THE CENTURY MAGAZINE, Vol. LVI, No. 6, October, 1898.

Banning, Captain William, and Banning, George Hugh, *Six Horses,* New York, London, 1928.

Bay of San Francisco, The, A History, Vol. 2, Chicago, 1892.

Bee's, Frederick A., Identification with the History of California, MS., Bancroft Library, University of California.

Berthold, Dr. Victor M., *William H. Russell, Originator and Developer of the Pony Express,* THE COLLECTORS' CLUB PHILATELIST, Vol. VII, Nos. 1 and 2, Fredericksburg, 1929.

Biggs, Donald C., *The Pony Express, Creation of the Legend,* San Francisco, 1956.

Boggs, Mae Helene Bacon, *My Playhouse Was a Concord Coach,* Oakland, Calif., 1949.

Bradley, Glenn D., *The Story of the Pony Express,* Chicago, 1913.

Buckland, Samuel S., *Indian Fighting in Nevada,* MS., Bancroft Library, University of California.

Burton, Richard F., *City of the Saints,* London, 1861.

Carter, William A., *Letter to John S. Jones, Leavenworth City, April 23, 1860,* Bancroft Library, University of California.

Chapman, Arthur, *The Men of the Pony Express,* THE PACIFIC MONTHLY, May, 1910.

—— *The Pony Express,* New York and London, 1932.

Chorpenning, George, *Map submitted with claim on United States Government* (n.d.), Bancroft Library, University of California.

Congressional Globe, The, Thirty-Sixth Congress, 2nd Session, Vol. II.

Conkling, Roscoe P. and Margaret B., *The Butterfield Overland Mail, 1857-1869*, Glendale, California, 1945.

Connelly, William Esley, *Doniphan's Expedition* (containing "Personal Recollections" by Charles R. Morehead, Jr.), Kansas City, 1907.

Contra Costa Gazette, The, Martinez, California.

Coy, Owen C., *The Pony Express Ante-dated*, THE GRIZZLY BEAR MAGAZINE, Vol. XX, No. 4, February, 1917.

Cross, Ralph Herbert, Sr., *The Early Inns of California*, San Francisco, 1954.

Daily Alta California, San Francisco.

Daily News, Placerville, California.

Davis, Samuel P. (Ed.), *History of Nevada*, 2 vols., Reno, Los Angeles, 1913.

Deseret News, Salt Lake City.

Dieker, Leo E., *Hollenberg Ranch Pony Express Station* (pamp., n.d.), Hanover, Kansas.

Driggs, Howard R., *The Pony Express Goes Through*, New York, 1935.

Egan, William M., (Ed. and Comp.) *Pioneering the West, 1846-1878*, Richmond, Utah, 1917.

Fairfield, Asa Merrill, *Fairfield's Pioneer History of Lassen County, California*, San Francisco, 1916.

Gove, Captain Jesse A., *The Utah Expedition*, Concord, New Hampshire, 1908

Gwin, William M., *Memoirs*, MS., Bancroft Library, University of California.

Hafen, Leroy R., *The Overland Mail to the Pacific Coast, 1848-1869*, (thesis) MS., Bancroft Library, University of California.
────── *The Overland Mail*, Cleveland, 1926.

Harlow, Alvin F., *Old Waybills*, New York, 1934.
────── *Old Wires and New Waves*, New York, London, 1936.

Harrington, Gerald F., *Map of Pony Express Trail*, blueprint copy in author's library, Oakland, 1935.

Hawthorne, Hildegarde, *Ox-Team Miracle, the Story of Alexander Majors*, New York, Toronto, 1942.

Hungerford, Edward, *Wells Fargo, Advancing the American Frontier*, New York, 1949.

Hutchings California Magazine, Vol. IV, October, 1859; Vol. V, July, 1860.

Inman, Henry, and Cody, Colonel William F., *The Great Salt Lake Trail,* New York, 1898.

James, George Wharton, *Heroes of California,* Boston, 1910.

Knapp, Edward S., *Pony Express* (pamp.), New York, 1936.

Latham, Hon. Milton S., *Remarks of Hon. Milton S. Latham of California on Overland Mails, U.S. Senate, May 30, 1860,* (pamp., n.d.).

Little, Feramorz, MS., Bancroft Library, University of California.

Loeb, Julius, *The Pony Express,* THE AMERICAN PHILATELIST, Vol. 44, No. 2, November, 1930.

Majors, Alexander, *Seventy Years on the Frontier,* Chicago, 1893.

Majors, Greene, MS., printed copy in California Historical Society, San Francisco.

Morgan, Dale L., *The Humboldt, Highroad of the West,* New York, 1943.

Mountain Democrat, Placerville, California.

National Intelligencer, Washington, D. C.

Nevada, A Guide to the Silver State, Portland, 1940.

Nevada Historical Society Papers, Reno.

Nevada Magazine, The, September, 1947.

New York Tribune

Oakland Tribune

Paxon, Frederic L., *History of the American Frontier,* New York, 1924.

Pony Express (western Americana monthly), Placerville, California.

Pony Express Collection, Wells Fargo Bank, History Room, San Francisco.

Rideing, William H., *History of the Express Business,* HARPER'S NEW MONTHLY MAGAZINE, Vol. LI, No. CCCIII, August 1875.

Roberson, Joseph S., *History of Wells, Fargo & Co. and the Pony Express,* MS., San Francisco, 1879, Huntington Library.

Root, Frank A., and Connelly, W. E. *The Overland Stage to California,* Topeka, 1901.

Russell, Majors & Waddell Papers, 1839-1868, Huntington Library.

Sacramento Union.

San Francisco Daily Globe.

San Francisco Evening Bulletin.

San Francisco Evening Gazette and Telegraph.

San Francisco Herald.

Scott, Edward B., *The Saga of Lake Tahoe*, Crystal Bay, Lake Tahoe, 1957.

Scrugham, James G. (Ed.), *Nevada, A Narrative of the Conquest of a Frontier Land*, Chicago and New York, 1935.

Settle, Raymond W. and Mary Lund, *Empire on Wheels*, Stanford, California, 1949.

————— *Saddle and Spurs, The Pony Express Saga*, Harrisburg, 1955.

Simpson, Captain J. H., *Report of Explorations Across the Great Basin of the Territory of Utah in 1859*, Washington, D. C., 1876.

Sioli, Paola (Comp.), *History of El Dorado County, California*, Oakland, 1883.

Society of California Pioneers Quarterly, Vol. II, No. 2, June, 1925.

Stimson, A. L., *History of the Express Business*, New York, 1881.

United States House of Representatives, Executive Document 71, Thirty-Fifth Congress, 1st Session.

United States House of Representatives, Report No. 78, Thirty-Sixth Congress, 2nd Session.

United States Senate Document No. 28, Thirty-Eighth Congress, 1st Session.

Utah Historical Society Quarterly, Vol. XXII, No. 1, January, 1954.

Thompson & West, *History of Nevada*, Oakland, 1881.

Visscher, William Lightfoot, *The Pony Express* (reprint), Chicago, 1946.

Westerns Brand Book, Los Angeles, 1947.

Western Horseman, The, Vol. VII, No. 1, January-February, 1942.

APPENDIX

Part I — Pony Express Stations

If the proprietors of the Pony Express had recorded a complete list of stations at which riders changed horses or relayed the mail— an improbable document—posterity would be gratefully indebted. To the contrary, it would seem that the division superintendents, left largely to their own devices, made arrangements as they saw fit at such places as convenience and distance required, being charged only with the responsibility of getting the express through. The result has been that any all-inclusive, accurate list has virtually defied compilation. Minor changes in route, place name differences and changes in stations themselves have complicated the effort. Oversight didn't help either. In June, 1861, Superintendent Buckley of the Overland Mail measured with an odometer the distances between stage stations from Fort Churchill to Sale Lake City, but paid no attention to Pony Express stations!

Two sources, however, are rich in station identification: Burton's *City of the Saints* and Harrington's *Map of Pony Express Trail*. It is by the generous aid of these, with emendations based on citations in numerous text references, that the following list is made. For easier interpretation, the arrangement ignores the borders of the contemporary Kansas, Nebraska and Utah Territories in favor of the present division of states.

MISSOURI
St. Joseph

KANSAS
Elwood
Cold Springs
Troy
Kennekuk
Granada
Log Chain
Seneca
Guittard's
Marysville
Cottonwood
  (Or Hollenberg's Ranch)

NEBRASKA
Rock Creek
Big Sandy
Thompson's
Kiowa
Little Blue
Liberty Farm
Lone Tree
32-Mile Creek
Summit
Fairfield
Hook's
Fort Kearny
Platte Station
Craig

NEBRASKA *(Cont'd)*

Seventeen Mile
Plum Creek
Willow Island Ranch
Cold Water Ranch
Midway
Gilman's Ranch
Cottonwood Springs
Junction House Ranch
Fremont Springs
O'Fallon's Bluff
  (Or Halfway House)
Elkhorn
Alkali Lake
Sand Hill
Beauvais Ranch
Diamond Springs

COLORADO

South Platte
Julesburg

NEBRASKA

Lodge Pole
30-Mile Ridge
Mud Springs
Courthouse Rock
Chimney Rock
Ash Hollow
Scott's Bluffs
Fort Mitchell

WYOMING

Spring Ranch
Torrington
Bedeau's Ranch
Fort Laramie
Ward's
  (Or Central Star)
Horseshoe Creek
LaBonte

WYOMING *(Cont'd)*

Orin
Douglas
Fetterman
Box Elder Creek
Deer Creek
Glenrock
Platte Bridge
  (Casper)
Red Buttes
Willow Springs
Sweetwater
Split Rock
Rock Creek
Three Crossings
Rocky Ridge
Horse Creek
Quaking Asp Creek
South Pass
Pacific Springs
Dry Sandy
Big Sandy
Green River
Ham's Fork
Millersville
Fort Bridger
Muddy Creek
Quaking Asp Springs
Bear River

UTAH

Needle Rocks
Weber
Carson House
Dixie Creek
Snyder's Mill
Big Canyon Creek
Salt Lake City
Traveler's Rest
Rockwell's
Joe's Dugout

UTAH *(Cont'd)*
Camp Floyd
  (Later, Fort Crittenden)
Rush Valley
Point Lookout
Egan's Springs
  (Or Simpson's Springs,
  Lost Springs)
River Bed
Dugway
Fish Springs
Boyd's
Canyon Station
Willow Springs
Deep Creek

NEVADA
Antelope Springs
Spring Valley
Schell Creek
Egan's Canyon
Butte
Mountain Springs
Ruby Valley
Jacob's Wells
Diamond Springs
Sulphur Springs
Roberts Creek
Camp Station
Dry Creek
Cape Horn
Simpson's Park
Reese River
Edwards Creek
Cold Springs
Sand Springs

NEVADA *(Cont'd)*
Stillwater
Sink of the Carson
Williams Station
  (Or Honey Lake Smith's)
Buckland's
Fort Churchill
Miller's Station
Reed's
Dayton
Carson City
Genoa
Friday's

CALIFORNIA
Woodford's
Lakeside
Yank's
Strawberry
Webster's
Moss
Sportsman Hall
Placerville
  *(El Dorado)
  (Mormon Tavern)
  (15-Mile House)
  (5-Mile House)
Pleasant Grove House
Folsom
Sacramento
Benicia
San Francisco

————

*Early route along White Rock road, followed until June, 1860, shown in parentheses.

Part II — Pony Express Riders

Among the straggling survivors to reach Buckland's Station after the bloody massacre at Pyramid Lake was a young ex-soldier from Camp Floyd. The ink was hardly dry on his honorable discharge from Company E of the 10th U. S. Infantry Regiment when he set out across the Nevada desert to join relatives in California. He got to Carson City at the same time word reached there of Monuannoga's grisly work at Williams' Station. Bartholemew Riley, evidently, was an adventurous spirit, for he easily was caught up in the hot wind of passion that swept through that frightened little town.

"As might be expected from a gallant soldier," a newspaper letter related a few days later, he threw in with the volunteers and marched with Major Ormsby. On the battlefield, "like the white plume of Henry of Navare, his course was where the battle raged fiercest and the bullets flew thickest, but he heeded them not." Winnemucca's cohort was made painfully aware of his unerring accuracy and "his friendly hands performed the last kind service for the lamented Ormsby."

It was written that Riley was among the last to leave the field, arriving at Buckland's about daybreak, just as the eastbound Pony rider reached the station from Carson City. The relief rider, shrinking from the performance of his duty, threatened failure of the express service. "Riley, fresh from the battlefield and tired as he was, stepped forth and volunteered to ride to the next change, a distance of 85 miles."

The following day, at the Cold Springs Station, the ex-soldier and expressman *pro tem* was wounded "by the acidental discharge of a weapon in the hands of a friend." Two weeks later, at Carson City, he died.

In attempting to compile a roster of Pony riders, this little vignette on Bartholemew Riley has double interest. First, vying for honors with Mark Twain's romanticized version of a Pony courier in *Roughing It*, it has that rare, valid quality of being a contemporary third-person account in commendable, if light, detail. Secondly, the time and circumstances of Riley's ride have a strange similarity to the famous trip of "Pony Bob" Haslam, which that worthy carefully related several decades later, with liberal use of the first person pronoun.

Too often, unfortunately, identification of individual expressmen rests on just such after-year exploit-telling, dimmed memories and artful scribes. Colorful work by the latter has turned out fabulous figures, like the 14-year-old rider, Bill Cody—which precocious lad, we are to believe, could outride them all. In the long letter of Salt Lake City businessman Jack Keetley, quoted by Visscher, we have a romantic and thrilling account of the ex-rider's own derring-do. Yet, luckily, his reminiscences help, as those of W. A. Cates and Tommy Ranahan told by Chapman, by the matter-of-fact mention of the names of other riders.

The whole problem lies with inadequate records of the day, so one needn't wonder that no two rosters of Pony expressmen ever jibe. They probably never will, as much as accuracy and completeness is strived for; too much has been forgotten.

With these handicaps, then, the following list is subjoined:

Henry Avis
Jim "Boston" Baughn
Melville Baughn
James Beatley
Charles Becker
Thomas J. Bedford
William Boulton
John Brandenburger
James W. Brink
Hugh Brown
Jimmy Bucklin
John Burnett
William Campbell
Alex Carlisle
William Carr
William Carrigan
W. A. Cates
Jimmy Clark
Richard W. Clark
"Deadwood Dick" Clarke
Richard Cleve
Charles Cliff
Gus Cliff
Wiliam F. Cody
James "Sawed Off Jim" Cumbo

Louis Dean
William Dennis
Thomas Dobson
Joe Donovan
W. E. Dorrington
Calvin Downs
James E. Dunlap
Major Howard Egan
Howard R. Egan
E. R. "Ras" Egan
J. K. Ellis
H. J. Faust
John Fisher
William F. Fisher
Thomas Flynn
Johnnie Fry
George Gardner
Jim Gentry
Jim Gilson
Sam Gilson
Frank Gould
William Hamilton
Robert "Pony Bob" Haslam
Martin Hogan
Lot Huntington

Charles Higgenbotham
William James
David R. Jay
Will D. Jenkins
Sam S. Jobe
Jack H. Keetley
Jay G. Kelley
Mike Kelley
Thomas O. King
John Koerner
Bob Martin
Sye Macaulas
Montgomery Maze
J. G. McCall
James McDonald
Pat McEarney
Jim McNaughton
William McNaughton
Charles B. Miller
Jim Moore
J. H. Murphy
George "Wash" Perkins
William Pridham
Thomas J. "Irish Tommy" Ranahan
Theodore Rand
James Randall
Thomas J. Reynolds
H. Richardson
Johnny Richardson

Bartholemew Riley
Don C. Rising
Harry L. Roff
C. H. Ruffin
Edward Rush
G. G. Sangiovani
John Seerbeck
John Sinclair
George Spurr
William H. Streeper
Robert C. Strickland
William Strohm
John W. Suggett
George Thatcher
Charles P. Thompson
James M. Thompson
George Towne
W. S. Tough
Warren Upson
William R. van Blaricon
Henry Wallace
Dan Wescott
Michael M. Whelan
James William
H. C. Willis
Nick Wilson
Barney Wintle
Henry Worley
Morse Wright
Jose Zowgalt

Appendix — Part III

CONTRACT FOR JOINT CARRIAGE OF MAIL
BETWEEN
CENTRAL OVERLAND CALIFORNIA & PIKES PEAK EXPRESS
AND
OVERLAND MAIL COMPANY*

This Memorandum of Contract—Witnesseth—That, whereas at the last session of the 36th Congress a law was passed authorizing the Postmaster Gen'l to make certain modifications in the contract for mail service on route 12,578—among others changing their route to what is known as the Central or Salt Lake Route—to be accepted by the contractors—

And whereas The Overland Mail Company now performing the service, and the recognized contractors on said Route, have accepted said modifications, and entered into a contract with the Postmaster General for the performance of service under said act of Congress —a copy of which contract is hereto appended and made part of this agreement. And whereas it has been agreed that "The Central Overland California & Pikes Peak Express Company" shall perform a part of said service. Now these Presents witness—That the said Express company, acting by Wm. H. Russell its President & duly authorized by its Board of Directors, party of the first part, and the said Overland Mail Company acting by Wm. B. Dinsmore its President, duly authorized by its Board of Directors, party of the second part, do mutually agree as follows.

1st.   Said first party agree to perform the entire service between the Eastern terminus and Salt Lake City, and to furnish facilities to accommodate the travel both "through" and "local"—The second party to perform the ballance [sic] of the service, and to afford like facilities, and to pay over to the first party quarterly as it shall be received from the Government & no sooner, mail pay at the rate of Four Hundred & Seventy Thousand Dollars per annum, after deducting therefrom one half the amt paid for sea service.

2nd.   The passenger business and the Express business to be divided as follows—The through passenger & through Express business to be divided equally—the local passenger & Express business

---

*[from manuscript copy at Huntington Library]

of first party to be divided seventy per cent to the first party and thirty per cent to the second party, and the local business of the second party to be retained by them entire. Settlements are to be made quarterly and all accounts ballanced [sic]. Business going only part way on both divisions charged as local & price to be fixed by the parties.

3rd.   Each party is to pay all fines occasioned by failures on their respective divisions. The division of time to be as follows — On the 20 day schedule the first party has 12 days and the 2nd party has 8 days. On the 23 day schedule the first party has 14 days & the 2nd party 9 days. And a like ratio on the 35 day schedule.

4th.   The receipt from Pony Express to be divided equally, each party as in carrying the mail paying their own expenses on their divisions.

5th.   A General Superintendent to be appointed by the second party, and paid equally by the two parties, shall have general charge and supervision of the Eastern line, so far as to see that the service is properly performed, but is not to interfere with the management and detail of the first party's division.

6th.   The Supt or other authorized agent of the second party shall have the right to examine the books of the first party in which are kept the accounts for this division. And an agent shall be kept at Ft. Kearney, paid equally by the parties who shall copy way bills & attend to the business of both parties.

7th.   The second party reserve the right and privilege of making an exclusive contract for the Express business with Wells Fargo & Co. for all business going from the East to any point West of Salt Lake City and for all business originating west of Salt Lake City going East—at a fair compensation—said business shall be called through business and divided as such.

8th.   In case any change or modification by Congress or the P.M. Gen'l of the said contract so as to deprive the 2nd party of the mail pay then the 2nd party are not to be held liable or responsible to the first party.

9th.   Whenever either party reaches the common point of Salt Lake City, the other party will proceed with the mail at once without waiting for the schedule time, and it is understood that the whole trip is to be made as rapidly & promptly as possible.

10th.   It is further stipulated and agreed that in case the 1st party should fail to perform their contract, and a serious interruption should take place, and if it should become necessary for the 2nd party to assume the performance of the entire service, then said second party shall have the right to at once take possession of the entire stock and equipments of the 1st party, and use the same in performing the service, and they shall have the right to and shall purchase said stock and equipment at an appraised value, each party selecting an appraiser, and the two an umpire (whose decision shall be final) if necessary.

As it is further expressly stipulated that in case said 1st party shall fail as aforesaid and the second party shall be obliged to perform the service, then said 1st party shall pay the sum of one hundred thousand dollars to the second party, which sum shall be liquidated damages and paid without deduction or offset.

In witness whereof the parties hereto have subscribed their names this 16th day of March 1861 at the City of New York.

Wm. H. Russell, Prest.
Interlineations on 2nd & 4th pages   *The C.O.C. & P.P. Ex. Co.*
made before signing
In presence of   W. B. Dinsmore, Prest.
Milton S. Latham   *Overland Mail Co.*

INDEX